The Missing Peace

The missing PEACE

SOLVING THE ANGER PROBLEM FOR ALCOHOLICS, ADDICTS AND THOSE WHO LOVE THEM

Sharing the Best-Kept Secrets in Psychology:
Emotional Regression and Working with
the Anger-Reducing Detour Method

JOHN LEE

Health Communications, Inc.
Deerfield Beach, Florida

www.hcibooks.com

Library of Congress Cataloging-in-Publication Data

Lee, John H.,m 1951-
    The missing peace : solving the anger problem for alcoholics, addicts and
those who love them . . . / John Lee
        p. cm.
    Contents: Contents: The anger problem—Rage is the real problem—The
solution–the beginning—Understanding emotional regression—The detour
method–the way out—Setting boundaries and knowing your limits—
Coming out of shock and into feeling—Now for the spiritual side.
    ISBN 0-7573-0423-0 (tp)
    1. Substance abuse—Treatment. 2. Substance abuse—Psychological
aspects. 3. Anger. I. Title

RC564.L435 2006
362.29—dc22

                                                               2005055063

HCI, its Logos and Marks are trademarks of Health Communications, Inc.

Publisher: Health Communications, Inc.
            3201 S.W. 15th Street
            Deerfield Beach, FL 33442-8190

Cover design by Larissa Hise Henoch
Inside book design by Lawna Patterson Oldfield

For my father, Jimmy;

my mother, Frances;

my brother, Randy;

my sister, Kathy;

and

my best friend/wife, Susan

CONTENTS

3 THE SOLUTION—THE BEGINNING

4 UNDERSTANDING EMOTIONAL REGRESSION

5 THE DETOUR METHOD—THE WAY OUT

6 SETTING BOUNDARIES AND KNOWING YOUR LIMITS

7 COMING OUT OF SHOCK AND INTO FEELING

8 NOW FOR THE SPIRITUAL SIDE

APPENDIX

ACKNOWLEDGMENTS

EVERY WRITER NEEDS A GOOD EDITOR. I have four I wish to thank—Allison Janse at HCI, my dear friend Bill Stott, who edits and supports my writing, Jennifer Hanawalt, and my dear wife Susan Lee.

I also wish to thank folks who contributed so much to my understanding of anger—Joe Laur, Dan Jones, James Redfield, Robert Bly, Karen Luzuis and many others, especially my clients and workshop participants.

Many heartfelt thanks to AA, Al-Anon, Adult Children of Alcoholics and Co-Dependents Anonymous for all they have taught me about anger and forgiveness.

And a special thanks to Peter Vegso for more than twenty years of publishing support.

PREFACE

THE MISSING PEACE TO RECOVERY details a significant recovery breakthrough that offers a lasting effect and helps men and women deal with a part of recovery that has been misunderstood, misquoted and just plain missing: **Anger.** *The Missing Peace to Recovery* will answer the recovering person's most frequently asked questions: "What do I do with my anger?" "Is it really okay to express it?" "Can I do so without hurting myself and others, and without risk of relapse?" The answer is "Yes, yes, yes!" Let's learn how to say yes to appropriately expressed anger, and yes to peace.

I am a recovering alcoholic who was raised in an extended family of alcoholics and drug addicts. I've been in recovery for twenty years, but not without a few slips. I have counseled alcoholics and addicts for twenty years. I have also listened to and worked with the people who love them, live with them, can't live without them, work with them, play with them and are exhausted by them. I have trained hundreds of therapists and counselors how to safely facilitate the appropriate expression of anger. Everyone wants a solution to the anger problem, but many psychologists and therapists are unable to provide one. This book provides the pieces that have been missing from many alcoholics' and addicts' recovery programs, and thus provides the peace we all want in our lives.

For years I tried to erase my anger and achieve this elusive thing called peace through meditation, prayer and intellect— but none of these was ever intended to make anger go away. They were just ways to bypass my feelings, not only of anger, but also of sadness, grief, loneliness, fear and even love. Much later I learned feelings are meant to be felt, not bypassed or ignored. I tried to convince myself and others that I was above such feelings and didn't really have them or need them. I was too smart and educated to be angry. As proof, I tried to write sensitive poetry and taught religious studies and meditation at the college level—all the while drinking, drugging and medicating to keep my feelings under wraps and peace at bay. I was wrapped a little too tightly for my own and others' comfort and safety.

I hit my bottom in 1985 and began to learn how to express past and present pent-up emotions. I wrote my first book, *The Flying Boy: Healing the Wounded Man*, which chronicled my personal journey from being "a head on a stick," as I used to refer to myself, to a man who began to try to heal all that had gone unfelt for so long. I began the long, arduous journey— the extremely long one—the eighteen inches from my head to my heart. What I found along the way was a great deal of sadness, a whole lot of unexpressed anger and ultimately a peace greater than anything I'd ever known. By learning how to release my rage and anger and get it out of my body, I found I no longer needed to medicate it with alcohol or drugs. I finally came home to my body and began to experience the serenity that accompanies being comfortable in your own skin.

I hope this book enables you to bring a little more peace into your life now that you are ready to explore the missing piece of most recovery programs.

(NOTE: *This book is not the suitable path for rageaholics who frequently hit, slap and use verbal abuse. These people must first learn to contain their rage, and much later learn how to express anger appropriately. This book is not for these folks, but for the 99 percent of the population who rage intermittently, occasionally, sporadically, once in a blue moon, but not every day.*)

1

THE ANGER PROBLEM

ALCOHOLICS/ADDICTS AND THE
PEOPLE WHO LOVE THEM ARE ANGRY

ALL ADDICTS HAVE EXPERIENCED unexpressed anger, or expressed it so inappropriately that the people around them have been hurt, irritated, frustrated, angry and even enraged with the disease. Most alcoholics have one thing in common: When they were growing up, anger caused everyone pain in some form or another. Even if they failed math, they learned one equation in their home: anger equals pain. That pain may come in the form of heartaches, abuse, abandonment, isolation, degradation, withdrawal, whippings, beatings and shaming. All of which hurt them or the ones they love. At some point most decided that if they just didn't get angry then no one would get hurt, including themselves. So they swallowed

their anger, stuffed it into their bodies like they were gunny-
sacks or body bags. Everyone denied anger's existence or
rationalized it away. Some smiled, stabbed people in the back,
sabotaged relationships, manipulated, sought revenge, con-
trolled, forgave prematurely, played nice, and got drunk,
stoned, high and numb. Resentments turned into thick bricks
and were used to build walls around themselves, but the anger
leaked out, in spite of the mortar, harming everyone in the
near vicinity. Alcoholics and addicts became *resentful*, a
luxury the alcoholic and addict cannot afford.

One of the key criticisms of Alcoholics Anonymous (AA),
Narcotics Anonymous (NA) and Al-Anon is that many participants are full of anger, even after being in recovery for
many years. They talk all the time about how their sponsor
"straightened my ass out" or "called me on my bullshit" or
"confronted me and set me straight." Confrontation, criticism
and put-downs of all kinds seem to be acceptable, but they
really make most alcoholics and addicts even angrier, though
they've learned to look and act like they aren't. As the Billy
Crystal character on *Saturday Night Live* used to say, "It's better to look good than to feel good."

I had been thinking for two or three years about writing
this book. One Saturday morning I attended my regular AA
meeting. Afterward I went to lunch with a bunch of folks who
talked about how angry a certain member was after twenty-
seven years of sobriety. I wondered if anyone else noticed our
own anger, which took the form of gossiping about that member's inappropriate expression of anger. That was when I realized how badly I needed to write this book, not only for others
but for myself as well.

ANGER IS JUST A FEELING

Anger is a feeling. It is one of the primary emotions like sadness, happiness, fear, loneliness and gratitude. It is not inherently negative, though if repressed long enough it can have negative consequences, ranging from headaches, stomachaches, and backaches to more serious things like colitis, insomnia, some say even cancer and heart disease. Repressed anger also hurts others when it takes the form of abuse, violence and mayhem. Yet anger is a natural response to life's unfairness, people's unkindness, and the sounds of leaf blowers and lawn mowers before 9 A.M. on an otherwise beautiful Sunday morning.

Anger is simply energy in the body that can be used to get us out of stuck places—marriages where the husband or wife is abusive, jobs that pay less than minimum wage but expect us to give 200 percent of ourselves. It can extricate us from unjust or unholy wars, oust presidents and help us get MADD about irresponsible drinkers. Intellect alone, without linking itself to anger, will seldom right wrongs. Anger is the energy to be used to get us out of stuck places.

EVERYONE GETS ANGRY

Anger is a persistent and universal problem mostly because no one taught us how to express it without hurting others or ourselves. No one can avoid it 100 percent of the time. It is a natural part of the human condition. The people we love the most are the people who most often trigger our anger. We get angry with our kids; our kids get angry with us. Many adults are still angry with their parents—even if the parents have been dead for twenty years. Husbands are angry with their wives for wanting more tenderness than they can muster; wives are angry with their husbands for thinking intimacy is two or three glorious minutes in the bedroom.

This pesky thing called anger just won't go away; it's the annoying little flea that bites humanity's butt. We all wish it were really that small; then it would be easier to squash or hide. All too often anger is the elephant in the living room: obvious and obtrusive—leaving a big mess to clean up after— yet no one talks about it.

WHERE DOES IT ALL BEGIN?

Like most things, anger begins in childhood. Children come into this world with a broad range of emotions ready to be felt—until someone tells them that they don't feel what they feel. "You're not angry." "Don't be mad." "You don't have anything to be angry about—you have it so much better than the children in Africa." Children experience early on that show- ing anger results in punishment. A client of mine, Jason, was told at age six that if he got angry his mother would "take me to the police station, turn me in and tell them to keep me."

Most families have one or two people who are allowed to get angry—usually these individuals do so in the most intim- idating or abusive manner. For example, most families have the stormy one, the seething one, the silent one, the destruc- tive one, the rebellious one, the overachiever, the "right" one and the "wrong" one, the one who leaves and the one who stays no matter how much that one would like to leave. Most people in recovery know that family members tend to assume certain roles: the "peacemakers," who are really more like referees and have very little if any peace in their own lives; the "hero," whose job it is to save the family and the family name and he or she is usually worn out by the time they are six from slaying family dragons; the "lost child," who never seems to be around and who is arguably the smartest of them all but who can never quite find his or her own way in the world; and finally, the "scapegoat," who carries the sins of the family on his or her back and is constantly being slaughtered with everyone's anger and rage.

We all know children don't take after strangers. You've never heard frustrated parents say to their child, "You are just like the mailman." What is modeled for children early on is what they rely on later in life. Adults learned verbal, physical and emotional behaviors that are abusive or inappropriate when they were children; they didn't suddenly invent them when they grew up. People who grow up in an alcoholic home almost never see anger expressed in a healthy manner. Consequently, as adults they must unlearn the old behaviors and learn and practice new, healthier ways of expressing anger. The question is where will they go to learn?

If a child is given three crayons with which to color, all his life he will use only those three crayons, thinking there are no other choices. Healthy individuals discover there are more options available. They learn how to use colored pencils and markers, and then graduate to painting on canvas. They must practice with their new tools and give up relying on the old.

Only then can they paint their lives the way they want.

Most of the men and women I have worked with have said, "I thought the way our family was, was the way all families were. I didn't know it could be different. Where do we go to learn?" Some reading this are unsure if they even have an anger problem. Many genuinely live with the assumption that it is their father, wife or child that has the problem. If they are the ones with the problem, then this book will help you; and if it is you who has the problem, then perhaps it will help them.

ANGER AS PUNISHMENT AND REVENGE

Alcoholics, addicts, and adult children of alcoholics and addicts don't get angry—they get even. One of the reasons adults have such a problem feeling and expressing their anger is because anger has forever been tied to punishment and revenge. People who are punished—instead of disciplined— tend to seek revenge and be angry. And the best way to extract a pound of flesh is to punish the actual or perceived offender. You drink—I'll show you—I won't sleep with you. If you overreact—I'll get you back—I'll have an affair.

A few years ago I was in the Asheville airport waiting to catch a flight back to Austin. I was standing close to an elderly woman who was sitting hunched over in a wheelchair in front of her sixty-something-year-old daughter and son. She was silently weeping and the son looked down at her and said in a voice loud enough for all around him to hear, "Momma, we told you if you cried we wouldn't let you come back to visit anymore." Do you hear the rage and revenge in his statement? "That's right, Mother. We told you that you can't cry," said the daughter. Can't you just imagine that fifty-something years ago this mother probably said to her children, in some public place, "If you don't stop this crying, I'm never going to. . . ."? She punished them with a threat. They waited fifty years for revenge, and no one is consciously being malicious.

THE DIFFERENCE BETWEEN DISCIPLINE AND PUNISHMENT

Unfortunately, children are punished and they become, using Alice Miller's words, "Prisoners of Childhood," the original title of her important book, later named *The Drama of the Gifted Child*. Punishment makes children, adults, criminals and animals untrusting at the least, and full of rage at the most. It is capricious—not well-thought-out and not stated before the fact. Where punishment is handed out, you might as well hand out the alcohol and drugs to make those punished forget that they have no choice and that others have extreme amounts of power over them.

One time I asked a room full of counselors, educators and law enforcers if they could tell me exactly what would happen to someone caught in their state driving while under the influence. A couple of them said, "They would go to jail." Another one said, "They would lose their license to drive." Two or three said they would have to pay a fine. But several said, "It would depend on who they are, who they know, if they could afford a high-priced attorney and, sadly, what color they are. A poor person of color, who doesn't know anyone, is punished differently than someone who is white and has lots of money or connections." Hear the meanness in this? How enraged is someone going to be?

Now, here is what makes people less angry: discipline.

Discipline is almost angelic compared to demonic punishment. Here's why. Punishment is after the fact or the offense. Discipline is before the act or offense. Punishment takes away healthy choice making. Discipline teaches how to make healthy and mature choices. Punishment says here are the consequences I, or we, feel like handing out today. Discipline says know beforehand what the consequences of your actions will be no matter how we do or don't feel today.

If my home state of Georgia had huge billboards on every road into the state saying exactly what the consequences would be for driving under the influence, say—YOU WILL LOSE YOUR LICENSE. YOU WILL GO TO JAIL. YOU WILL PAY $10,999 IN FINES. AND, WE WILL CUT OFF YOUR BIG TOE—many folks would "think before they drink." Or they'd think, "Damn, if they're going to be so clear, I'll just go to Alabama where the law is still ambiguous as hell and take my chances over there."

It is the same with children and adolescents who are disciplined rather than punished. They just don't tend to be as angry and have to get even later with their guards—I mean parents and teachers—because they were told what would happen beforehand. One time my stepdaughter, who was about thirteen at the time, came in one warm summer evening very late, having been with her girlfriends chatting and forgetting about the time. As soon as she came through the door she looked at me in disgust and said, "I know, I'm busted for staying out so late." The anger at being punished many times by her real father was on her face as she prepared to get more. "Did I tell you what would happen before you went out if you weren't in by 9 P.M.?" She looked at me like I was asking her a trick question. She sighed heavily as all teenagers do. "No, you didn't." "Well, that's my job—to tell you beforehand the consequences so you can make choices. So, no, you're not busted. However, if you decide to stay out late again tomorrow night, you won't attend the sleepover this weekend with your girlfriends." I'll never forget what she said: "That sounds fair." And it was.

Punishment takes no time and is fast and very often furious. Discipline takes time and forethought. Punishment creates rage, resentment and the need for revenge and retribution. Discipline creates a sense of well-being and a feeling that one is cared for. All the young and older children I've seen and spoken with and all the adults have incredibly angry stories about being punished; almost none have stories of being disciplined.

Here's a little sidebar to all of this. The only institution that at least tries to practice discipline is—would you believe?—the military. They have huge books of rules and regulations: If you go AWOL—this, this and this will happen. If you disregard a direct order—this, this and this will happen. It is spelled out beforehand. You can actually look up what is going to happen should you violate the rules.

The bottom line: if you want to produce less angry children who become less angry adolescents who will then become less angry adults who feel safe, loved and valued in this world, learn to discipline instead of punish. May I suggest a useful book: *Positive Discipline: A–Z*, by Jane Nelsen, Lynn Lott and H. Stephen Glenn. Angry adults need to drink and drug to forget how punishment caused them *not* to feel safe, loved and valued in this world. Punishment just royally pisses off everyone, and then out roll the resentments, and out rolls the beer and whiskey barrels that are, at first, a barrel of fun and laughter, but eventually become containers of poison that kill families, friendships, opportunities and relationships of all kinds.

How to Know If You Have an Anger Problem

1. People often say you are angry—especially the people who know you well.
2. When you get angry, it's always someone else's fault. (The kids are being too noisy, your spouse is late again, the boss didn't appreciate the work you did, etc.)
3. People tell you to lighten up, relax, take it easy, have a drink or try a Valium.
4. You drink alcoholically, take drugs, or engage in addictive or dangerous behaviors.
5. You become angry while driving; this includes pointing at another driver with the middle finger or cutting off another car.
6. You hit your children, your spouse or animals. Hitting can be accomplished with many different weapons, not just the hands. Whether you use your hands, abusive words or a belt, get immediate professional help.
7. You have a rigid body structure; your neck and shoulders are tight and sore.

8. You have ulcers, insomnia, high blood pressure or frequent tension headaches.
9. You always have to win arguments or get in the last word.
10. You find yourself sleeping in a different bed than your spouse.
11. You act out of anger without stopping to think how your words or actions will affect other people.
12. You have multiple divorces.
13. When someone makes you angry, you emotionally withdraw or give him or her the silent treatment.
14. When someone hurts you, you become obsessed with hurting him or her back. You may even take pride in your ability to get even.
15. Forgiveness is almost impossible.
16. You never say you are sorry, except in a sarcastic voice.
17. Reading this list makes you angry.

MISLEADING INFORMATION ABOUT ANGER

Many psychologists and counselors are confused about this most misunderstood emotion. One of the main reasons for this gross misunderstanding is the fact that these learned men and women are still confusing anger with rage. Once we stop using these words interchangeably, then anger will no longer be the crazy uncle in the family of feelings and thus will no longer need to be avoided.

Expressing Anger Creates More Anger

Some well-intentioned psychiatrists, psychologists, therapists and spiritual leaders claim that letting out our anger
creates and perpetuates more anger. This is true only if the
person is a continuous rageaholic, which the majority of
people are not. Most people in this country are repressives
who may rage sporadically. Most of these well-intentioned
critics are afraid of anger, both their own and other people's,
so they have a vested interest in their clients suppressing
their anger. If a grieving man cries gallons of tears, it doesn't
make him cry even more. He weeps until the water in his
grief well is dry, and then he stops. A woman doesn't avoid
laughing at a joke because she is afraid she'll never stop
laughing! When allowed to run its natural course, every
emotion has an end. If I release a pound of pent-up anger at
my alcoholic father, then I don't have to release that same
pound again; I'll go on to feel and release the next pound of
anger until it is all gone.

Expressing Anger Is Dangerous

Some people who are anger-phobic claim getting angry
increases the blood pressure and strains the heart. In twenty
years of facilitating the appropriate release of anger for thousands of people, I've never seen anyone die from high blood
pressure or stroke at an anger workshop. However, I bet you
have known someone who died full of anger, and you were
sure their high blood pressure and heart disease were caused
by all those years of pent-up emotions. I'm not a physician,

but I can tell you that for the years I have practiced the methods discussed in this book, I've seen thousands of people express and release their anger, then celebrate as their blood pressure went down. They slept better, medicated less often, ground their teeth less, had fewer nightmares, and felt and expressed love more readily. Indeed, they felt much better for finally being allowed to express their feelings and get them out of their bodies.

Anger Is a Chameleon

Most genuinely compassionate psychologists believe anger is a secondary emotion and, therefore, not even real. What we are really feeling, they tell us, is not anger at all, but fear or sadness, depending on the therapist's personal history and training. Remember, therapists are people too, people who learned that anger equals pain, just like you and I did. They may encourage you to "understand" your anger or "go for the feeling that anger is covering up." At best, they tell you "to say more about this." Most will not tell you to feel it and express it—unless they have done some anger work themselves. Unless they have experienced and expressed their own anger, they will tend to tell you to "dance with it," forget it, move on or get over it. These are all intellectual ways of avoiding anger, which we will discuss shortly. Only a handful of professionals will tell you to face it, feel it, express it and release it.

Anger Is a Deadly Sin

Some religious counselors consider anger one of the "seven deadly sins." Now that should make you wary—anger is "deadly" *and* a "sin"! They conveniently ignore the instances in the New Testament where Jesus gets angry, such as the time when he encounters the moneychangers in his holy temple. He doesn't sit down with these scalawags, try to "interface" with them or mirror back to them what they are saying, and ask them to do the same. He kicks their butts, turns over some tables and cracks a whip. If Jesus never sinned, then anger is not a sin. What some religious people do with their anger, however, is a whole different ballgame. Do you remember when basketball wasn't an angry contact sport? How about that time you went to a hockey game and a fight broke out?

Forgive and Forget

Another misconception often pervasive among religious groups is that people must instantly offer forgiveness when someone harms them. It's a lofty goal, but beyond the capacity of the average mortal. For many, forgiveness can only be given after the feelings of anger, hurt and injustice have been addressed and worked through. Otherwise, the person can only offer premature forgiveness, a superficial remedy that never deals with the real problem.

The Bible says to turn the other cheek if someone slaps us, but it doesn't tell us what to do after being slapped twice. I believe it is okay to get angry and move out of the slapper's range. After all, sometimes anger's purpose is to get us out of threatening or unsafe places.

Do a Step on It

I position this section squarely between the religious and intellectual sections because it is a combination of both. Old-time Twelve Steppers will tell newcomers to "turn their anger over," "let go and let God," "do a step on it," or "make a gratitude list." All of these are great things to say when appropriate, but often these phrases are code for "don't feel your feelings—especially anger." Most recovering alcoholics and addicts are as afraid of anger as anyone else is. They too have been taught that anger equals pain.

An Avoidable Evil

The intellectual person tries to think away his or her feelings of anger, sadness, loneliness, fear or anxiety. Most of these people are so cut off from their bodies they wouldn't know a feeling if it bit them on the butt. I should know since I was a classic pseudo-intellectual escape artist. I was always flying up into my head so I wouldn't have to feel. When people asked me what I was feeling, I'd invariably tell them what I was *thinking*.

Intellectuals think they are too smart to stoop to the level of being angry, because emotions are primitive and illogical. They believe anger is an avoidable evil and should be omitted from any rational relationship.

Caution: Danger Zone

Bill was a client who had been married and divorced four times. When his wives were angry he used to say to them, "Now just calm down. We can discuss this like two intelligent people. If you don't calm down right now, I'm out of here." What was wrong with Bill trying to calm them down so they could discuss the matter? The ex-wives just wanted to feel their feelings and express them—it's called communicating. Bill interpreted their normal expressions of anger as a threat, because he associated anger with being hurt. In order to feel safe, he tried to shut down their anger. Bill was six feet tall and weighed two hundred pounds, but when someone near him got angry, he felt as small and helpless as he had when he was a small boy.

Don't Feel!

Most alcoholics and addicts learned at an early age not to show their feelings. Many men and women are embarrassed by their emotions and avoid displaying them in public at all costs. If they happen to cry in public, they immediately apologize or run for the bathroom until they regain control. Many of the men I've worked with over the last twenty years have said things like my last client, Bob: "I haven't cried publicly since I was seven years old." Bob is now sixty-five. Many men have bought the lie, "Big boys don't cry." I didn't cry in front of people until I was thirty-three.

Nice Girls Don't Get Angry

Many women are afraid to display anger because they were told: "It's not nice, " "It's not pretty," "It's not polite," "Angry people are ugly," and "Good girls don't get angry." They have been called "ballbusters" and "bitches." Women have just as much right to their anger as anyone. I repeat, women have lots of reasons to be angry. Hell, they weren't counted as a full person with the right to vote until 1920, and they still get paid two-thirds of what men do for the same jobs.

Alcoholism/addiction, among other things, is rage acted out by people who have been angry for a long time and who have been encouraged not to feel it, threatened not to feel it and, thus, are afraid to feel it. Most alcoholics and addicts have a lot of anger about how different they are, things are, situations are and people are, as opposed to the way they want themselves, others and situations to be. There is a huge space between what we want to be and what is, and that space is filled with alcohol and drugs, people and processes. That space between the way it is and the way we would like for it to be could be filled instead with anger, grief, acceptance and then love. However, most of us, as has been said, were not taught how to express our anger, or how to "accept" people, places and things as they are. So we drink and drug in lieu of this acceptance, and we may get very pissed off.

THE MANY FACES OF ANGER

Anger has more faces than Eve and more personalities than Sybil. Anger smiles at us while seething; it looks nice, forgiving and even sanctified. Anger's face is smeared with the hideous makeup of sarcasm. Out of anger's mouth come racist and sexist jokes and cruel put-downs. Anger is two-faced, tells stories and tales, and gossips behind our backs. Ultimately, our face betrays who we really are and that we are all angry to some degree.

WHAT ADDICTS DO WITH THEIR ANGER

Alcoholics drink away their anger, at least temporarily. If we put enough "spirits" in the body, we can make ourselves forget we have a spirit. We can make ourselves forget what we have done to our own bodies, what was done to our bodies and what we have done to other people's bodies, not to mention to our souls and their souls. But the pain doesn't go away; it just lies in wait like a crouching tiger but it's really a dangerous hidden dragon. We might be on an airplane when a father yells at his crying child, and we get so angry we want to go tell this terrible parent to jump without a parachute. Hearing that angry parent triggers our emotional memory. Alcoholics will avoid the emotions by asking the flight attendant for some bottles of Jack Daniel's or Smirnoff to tide them over until the baby stops crying, the plane lands, or we get too drunk and numb to care.

Sadly, alcoholics and addicts go to great extremes to comfort and numb themselves—drinking until their feelings fade into the distance, putting substances into their veins until sadness, anger and fear subside—all to keep the pain of their lives at bay.

And what about those folks who don't do crack, smack, dope or blow? How do they avoid their feelings? They fall in love with those who have the disease, marry them and become addicted to them and their bizarre behaviors.

THE ANGRY SPOUSE, CHILD
AND OTHERS WHO LIVE WITH ADDICTS

Everyone who lives with or loves an alcoholic or addict is a little insane. They have to be for a variety of reasons. If you read the Big Book of AA, you see many reasons why:

1. "Our homes have been battlegrounds many an evening."
2. "We seldom had friends at our homes, never knowing how or when the men in the house would appear. . . . We came to live almost alone."
3. "There was never financial security. Positions were always in jeopardy or gone. An armored car would not have brought the pay envelopes home."
4. "Sometimes there were other women."
5. "We have tried to hold the love of our children for their father. We have told small tots that father was sick. . . ."
6. "They struck the children, kicked out door panels, smashed treasured crockery, and ripped the keys out of pianos."
7. "In desperation, we have even got tight ourselves—the drunk to end all drunks."
8. "Usually we did not leave. We stayed on and on."
9. "For a while they would be their old sweet selves, only

to dash the new structure of affection to pieces once more."

10. "A body badly burned by alcohol does not recover overnight nor do twisted thinking and depression vanish in a twinkling."

These quotes were taken from the chapter "To Wives and The Family Afterward," but as we all know now, not only women have to suffer these things. Men have to live with alcoholic/addict wives, girlfriends and same sex partners as well. Whether they believe it or not, have a choice though the children do not. In the chapter "The Family Afterward" . . . in the Big Book, a "the sober mates doctor said to us, 'Years of living with an alcoholic is almost sure to make any wife or child neurotic. The entire family is, to some extent, ill.'" This important, life-changing book goes on to say, "The alcoholic may find it hard to re-establish friendly relations with his children. Their young minds were impressionable while he was drinking. Without saying so, they may cordially [*this is an understatement—my words*] hate him for what he has done to them and their mother." This "hate" may go on for years given the statistical fact that conservative estimates say that 50 percent of all adult children of alcoholics will either become alcoholics or addicts or marry one. More realistic studies say 80 percent.

There are many more reasons for loved ones to be angry that are not really discussed in the Big Book. The highs and lows of alcoholics and addicts keep everyone off balance and uncertain. One minute the addict is echoing the words of addict/guitarist Jimi Hendrix—"Excuse me while I kiss the sky." The next addicts are down so low that they feel they will never get up again and agree with the Allman Brothers, " . . . tied to a whipping post . . . Good Lord I feel like I'm dying."

With the highs and lows comes the inevitable incongruent behavior. They say one thing and do another. An alcoholic's or addict's words and actions almost never match. Unfortunately, those that were raised in a home of addiction become attracted and involved with people who never seem to follow through. We seem to be driven to be with people who seem "familiar." After all, the word familiar comes from the same root word as family.

So children of addicts live with the lies and the broken promises. They see the affairs and they watch those they love slowly kill themselves, all the while never feeling safe. They watch their father's or mother's health deteriorate with liver failure, high blood pressure, overdose and coma. They say, "I'll never be like them . . . I'll never be like them . . . Oh, my God, I'm just like them," or "I have married one of them." Those who love alcoholics are under constant tension and stress and then develop unhealthy ways to cope with it—usually involving some of the same things their parents or partners use to deal with the repressed rage, anger, sadness and other feelings they are too afraid to feel and express.

Here are a few other ways people avoid anger.

Work

They work seventy or eighty hours a week. The few hours they aren't working they are so tired they can't feel a thing from their heads down to their toes. This kind of addiction can be particularly appealing since it is endorsed by our

Protestant, or perhaps simply put, our "American Dream" work ethic.

Nicotine

Nicotine is the most lethal legal drug on the market today. While not as many smoke away, chew away or sniff away their feelings as they did fifty years ago, many still do. They take a feeling that lives in their chests and put a pack or two a day in there. It's like taking a syringe full of Novocain and sticking it right into the lungs and heart. They won't feel much of anything, until they are dying of cancer. If you are old enough, you might recall seeing people in the movies or on television right after making love reach over to the nightstand for their cigarettes and light up. It looked so relaxing, so cool, so like the thing to do—didn't it? Making love is one of the best feelings a man or woman can have. It is a way to open to the love that surrounds us and enfolds us. However, this love may open our bodies to what feels like too much intimacy, or to memories of other not so pleasant feelings, so we numb it back down to its usual state.

Caffeine

Caffeine is even more available to the public. Starbucks has seen to this, with a caffeine mainlining center on every corner (which I love, by the way). Give us a double shot of espresso and we're not going to feel much of anything for a while. It's legal, tastes good and is socially acceptable—what more could a recovering addict like myself want from a drug?

If you should visit any AA meeting in any part of the world you will see a coffee cup strapped to people's sides, at the ready to medicate any feeling that might come up during a meeting. Lovers of addicts and alcoholics love caffeine too, for exactly the same reasons.

Sugar

Sugar is the other legal "number" of feelings, and a drug that we Americans eat by the tons. Everything we eat has sugar in it—ketchup, soup, and the obvious pastries, cookies and candy—and alcoholics live for this stuff, as do many who don't qualify. Sugar takes the blues away temporarily and then drops us further down the depression scale an hour later. Sugar goes into the mouth and satisfies temporarily with the sweetness that living with an alcoholic or addict certainly doesn't provide. We start early. Our parents gave us sugar to comfort, console, pacify and babysit us—in lieu of attention, tenderness and affection—because many of them were too tired from workaholism or from paying attention to the alcoholic or addict, which is a full-time job just by itself.

Sex

Sex is legal in most states, with the possible exception of my home state, Alabama. Sex addiction is rampant in this country and can numb a feeling in a New York minute. Just like other addicts, sexaholics escape their histories, their present and their future by acting out their obsessions. There are also the love addicts, relationship addicts and flaming co-dependents who depend on pleasing people into thinking well of them to the point of exhaustion. All are angry, sad, scared, lonely, hurting folks, and if nothing else, they are angry at their diseases and all these manifestations of numbing feelings have to be dealt with sooner or later. But in the meantime, what do we do with our anger when the alcohol and addictions stop working and when a feeling of anger comes out in spite of all our best efforts? When traditions and teachings, religions and brains fail to numb our bodies? Anger is expressed inappropriately. We do this by employing one of four styles of **rage**.

2

RAGE IS THE REAL PROBLEM

THE FOUR MAIN STYLES OF RAGE

ALMOST EVERYONE—ADDICTS, ALCOHOLICS and those who love them—has a unique style of cooking, working and vacationing, and everyone has their own unique style of raging. Most choose a style unconsciously, of course, but as I've said before, "Children don't take after strangers." So we tend to choose a style of rage that gives us the illusion of control and a momentary feeling of power. Most of us also employ a style that works best in each regressive situation.

To use an example: Tom is a huge man by any standard. He is six feet, five inches tall and weighs over two hundred pounds. He confessed that when he is very angry with his wife he becomes the "intimidator," but with his teenage son he becomes the "interrogator," with his aging father the "distancer," and with his chronically ill mother the "poor pitiful me."

You have to get to the style you like the most, before the other person gets to it first. Physics says that "two bodies cannot occupy the same space." You never see two distancers, two interrogators or two intimidators at the same time, and two poor-me's are a pitiful sight no one wants ever to see.

All of the rage behaviors discussed below are sabotaging, controlling and manipulative. We employ them because they were shown to us at an early age. We watched to see who "won," "came out better," or "got their way," and which behavior looked better, stronger and more right. Remember, all these styles are *rage*, which is defined as "a behavior or action used to numb our feelings"—real feelings, like anger.

Intimidator

The intimidator is the man or woman who may get so loud and verbally abusive that the other person immediately feels very small and as if struck with words. Or the intimidator may get so silent and the silence so unbearable that the other person feels very afraid. The intimidator may yell, throw things, slam doors, squeal tires and gesture like a bad actor in the tragic comedy of alcoholism and addiction. This man or woman can threaten with the "look that could kill"—without ever saying a word. They engage in the "silent treatment" for hours, days, weeks, months and even years.

Intimidators put you down, criticize you, tell jokes at your expense, use their verbal or intellectual skills to put you on the defensive and embarrass you in front of others.

One time my father asked me to take him to play golf. Unable to express my anger appropriately back then, I replied, "Well, you know what Mark Twain said about golf?" My dad is a blue-collar worker who wasn't sure who Mark Twain was.

"No, what did he say?" He was not about to admit his ignorance to his college-educated son.

"That golf is a good walk spoiled."

Now, some people could say this to each other and laugh over a good joke. In my case, this remark was meant to hurt because I could not tell my father directly that I was still harboring some anger toward him, and he knew it. It's the kind of stuff intimidators do and then rationalize by saying, "Just kidding."

If the victim should attempt to stand up for him- or herself, all too often an intimidator will respond with an even more vicious assault. The intimidator's self-esteem rests on his or her feeling of power over others, and if they allow someone else to "win," or to admit their own faults, the playing field is leveled and their power is gone.

By the way, I've long regretted that comment I made to my father. The minute or two of silence between us reverberated with his disappointment. Were he to ask again, I'd go because, since then, I have confronted him directly about some past emotional injuries.

Interrogator

The interrogator was a member of the gestapo in a previous life. Interrogators only know how to fire rapid questions at their prisoner—I mean their partner or child: "Where were you?" "What time did I tell you to be home?" "Who were you with?" "Didn't I tell you I didn't want you hanging around with those other congressmen?" "How many more times have I got to tell you?" "Do you have an acceptable alibi?" "When are you going to go into therapy?"

Interrogators assault with their questions, they shine a bright light into your eyes, they slowly drip water on your head until you talk, and if that doesn't work, they will put bamboo shoots under your fingernails. They have many ways to make you talk.

Nancy, a good friend of mine, dated a man named Frank. He constantly put her down and made fun of her weight, makeup and clothes. One day she responded, "Who do you think you are? What gives you the right to criticize me? Have you looked at yourself in the mirror lately? How many beauty contests have you won?"

Right or wrong, Nancy gutted Frank using the sharp, cutting knife of questions.

Distancer

Then there are the distancers. These angry men and women always have one foot pointing toward the nearest door. They use one of the foulest four-letter words in the English language just before they leave—*fine*. "If you want to have your little tantrum—fine, I'm out of here." "Didn't we agree when we got married that there would be no expression of feelings and didn't you sign an agreement to this effect? Fine—break your agreement and see if you pry a feeling out of me." Even when the distancer doesn't physically leave, they leave emotionally—and you are talking to air. They are gone. They get in their car and, just for good measure, don't tell you where they are going, when they will be back and with whom they will be. You will get little, if any, information out of them unless you have honed your own interrogation skills.

Barbara is a distancer. Whenever she finds herself getting close to male or female friends, the fear of intimacy drives her into "distancer mode." If you call her, she won't call back, but when you see her at the supermarket she smiles and says, "I never got your message" or "My dog ate my answering machine."

Poor-Me

Last but not least, poor pitiful me has as much anger as anyone else but looks more martyrish than mad, more priestly than pissed off. Poor-me's really believe that nothing is their fault and the world just happens to not like them very much. The poor-me shows up to his anniversary party three hours late and tries to explain how he had every good intention of being there on time, but he had to take his clients to dinner and then to drinks afterward: "You know that is a part of my job to entertain clients. And then they wanted to fly to Japan and I couldn't get a direct flight back home in time so don't be angry at me, be angry at them. As a matter of fact let's go find them and you can kick their ass. I'll point them out to you, but believe me, it wasn't my fault and I'll never do it again. I promise."

RAGE: THINKING WE ARE EXPRESSING OUR ANGER AND SHARING OUR TRUE FEELINGS

Many people have been taught, especially since the sixties, that we are not supposed to hold in our feelings. We are to "confront" or "encounter" them, or have someone "call us on our stuff." This was a movement in the right direction, but most people do not feel safe around any of these behaviors.

Here are some other unhealthy ways anger is expressed.

Manipulation

Manipulating people is by far one of the more obvious ways anger leaks out, usually unknowingly. When we are angry we manipulate those around us, which gives us a momentary sense of power, which is the opposite of feeling angry because this feeling in others or ourselves usually left us feeling powerless.

Jim was angry, to say the least, at his wife, whom he felt did not appreciate the way he worked all the time to "keep her in the style that she had grown accustomed to as a child." So he would attend social functions by himself although both had been invited. He would convince her that she wouldn't enjoy the place or the people he associated with and that she would be much happier staying at home. Jim would then drink too much and flirt with every woman there.

Control

Control is the kissing cousin of manipulation. Angry people are usually very controlling people. They try to control people, places and things. They are like giant chess players moving the pawns around the board, partly because they are bored, but mostly because they are angry and just do not know it. Sometimes they make very subtle moves.

We had a housekeeper who felt she should be doing more in this world with her life and was really too smart to clean toilets. So she was angry, not with my wife and I per se, but at the circumstances of her life. She would rearrange everything in and on our desks, counters, closets and cabinets and end up hiding things. Then we would spend hours looking for them.

Jackie's mother always had to drive when she was in the car and if someone else said they wanted to, then she would change her mind at the last minute about going unless they agreed to let her pilot the car.

Jason refused to let his wife pay the bills, telling her that it was "a man's job."

Robin insisted her son of seven years play soccer, so he could learn discipline, even though he didn't want to. She kept telling him that someday he would thank her.

Robert gave his wife an allowance each week as a way to keep Beth from spending their money on cocaine. He checked the odometer in her car each evening to see if she used more than her allotted miles to go to the grocery store or pick up the children from school. When asked about this he said he was just helping his wife not use.

Sabotage

Sabotage is another cousin to manipulation and control. An example: Rodney's mother abandoned him when he was ten years old. She ran off with the minister of her church and he didn't hear from her again until he was twenty-eight years old. He was angry with her for leaving him with his alcoholic father, who was never there for him emotionally. In every relationship Rodney got into, he undermined his success, expressing his anger at women inappropriately and sabotaging all hopes of having a healthy relationship. Just when things were beginning to go deeper with a woman, he would withdraw from her emotionally, shut down, and next thing, he'd be involved with another woman before he ran off the current one.

Jokes

Telling really off-color, demeaning jokes is another form of anger leaking out of our overpressurized boilers. People who tell jokes about other races or gay people are really people who are pissed off about something. Many of you reading this right now may be ready to stop, thinking I'm trying to be politically correct or I'm a little anal retentive. Before you stop reading, put yourself in these people's places and imagine how you would feel if you were called some of those demeaning names. Probably angry. One of the ways these angry, put-down people justify their verbal punches is to throw out the outworn phrase, "I'm just joking."

Almost everyone has had a friend who puts him or her down. Bill had a wife who would put him down in public and then right after doing so would always add, "I'm just kidding. He knows I love him." Here in the South we have the ability to say anything nasty we want to about someone as long as we add at the end of it, "Bless his heart." For example: "Sherry is the worst mother in the world. She doesn't bathe that child of hers, she drinks all day long and ain't got the sense God gave a billy goat—bless her heart."

Shaming

Shaming folks is done so frequently we hardly even notice it, though we feel it engulfing our bodies like the toxic ooze it really is.

Jim's father would try to show him how to build things. When Jim wouldn't catch on fast enough, his father would say, "You can't be my son. We must have gotten the wrong baby at the hospital. My son would be able to fix or build anything, just like I do."

"What do you know? You were raised in the sticks," Tom's wife said when she was angry.

"Your feet are too big for your little body," Beth Ann often heard from her father.

"Shame on you," Lisa's mother often told her.

Blaming

Blaming is employed when folks are angry. They use statements like "It's all your fault," or "Look at what you've done now."

"We wouldn't be in this mess now if you had gotten that job in New York," Robin told her husband in my consulting room as they fought about finances. Jessie said to her husband George as she was packing up to leave him, "If you had gone with me to counseling like I asked you to years ago, we wouldn't be getting a divorce now."

Demeaning

"Look at how your mother raised you," said Robert to his daughter about his ex-wife.

"Can't you tell time? When the big hand is on twelve and the little hand is on twelve, that's when we meet for lunch," I sarcastically said to a girlfriend decades ago while confronting her about constantly being late for engagements.

Demoralizing

Demoralizing comes in different disguises. "Your brother is the one with the brains in this family." "I don't think you're ever going to understand me." "Men are pigs—bless their hearts."

Criticizing

Criticizing is so common that most of us actually think it's okay to receive or give it whether it's asked for or not. In my book *Facing the Fire: Experiencing and Expressing Anger Appropriately*, I have a chapter called "Saying No to Criticism," and this chapter has received more comments than all the others combined. One time I was on a radio talk show in Santa Fe and a psychiatrist called in and said he had read the chapter and wanted to ask a question:

"You mean to tell me that if I knew something that would make you a better writer, you wouldn't want me to tell you?"

"Not unless I asked you to."

"And if I knew how to help you become a better speaker, you wouldn't want me to tell you?"

"Not unless I invited you to do so."

"Then I'm willing to make a diagnosis right now: You are psychotic."

Do you think he might have been a little angry?

Most folks know way down deep in their guts that unsolicited criticism, even the kind that "is for their own good," or given "because I love you" stings like a thousand bees. As we pull the stingers out, our critics wonder what is wrong with us for taking it so badly; after all, we were just given "constructive criticism."

Unless I ask you to give me your opinion, feedback, input or, yes, criticism, it's only going to make me angry. If I open the door and ask, I'll almost always thank you for your honest comments. For example, before I get ready to send this book to my publisher, I will ask a half dozen people to tear it apart and tell me what doesn't work. But after it is edited, printed, released and received, I don't want to hear negative things about my paper-and-ink child or what you think I "should have done" to make it better. Which sounds a little like the next thing people do when they think they are expressing their anger.

Preaching

Preaching "the gospel according to you" is a familiar approach to releasing anger, especially for Southerners who grew up always within earshot of a pulpit and an angry preacher pounding out his rage to those in the pews—who believe he is talking straight to them while damning everyone to an eternity of hellfire and brimstone. Alcoholics and addicts and the people who love them preach to each other very often: "If you would only . . ."; "Why don't you pray more about it . . ."; "If you would only turn it over to your Higher Power . . ."; "I know the right way . . ." or "I'll be praying for you every day . . ."—which is more of a censure than a loving offer.

Teaching

You take want-to-be preachers and send them to college and give them a little knowledge and mix that with a few years of living with an alcoholic and you have **teachers** who are slightly subtler in the way they try to get their messages across. These angry folks tend to read self-help and recovery books addictively, underlining or highlighting in obnoxious pink or yellow markers everything they read because they know it applies to you. Then equally as subtly, they leave the book lying on the counter or on your pillow open to the page that most clearly shows who is the real problem, all the while thinking they are just being helpful.

Judging

The greatest of all these so-called helpers is the judge. These are angry men or women who think they are telling someone how they feel but who are really judging their actions, behaviors, motivations, character and personality. In reality, they are telling the person they are angry at more about them than they are about how they feel. The good judge gets to play two other roles for the price of playing the one—he or she also gets to be jury and executioner. These judges get to find the others guilty beyond a shadow of a doubt *and* impose the sentence they see fitting to the crime. An example: "I find you guilty of being an addict, bad husband and terrible father, and I sentence you to a lifetime of me telling you so every day, but I want you to know I'm not angry. You must be punished for the crimes you have committed against me and your family."

Analyzing

"Now that I have analyzed you, delved deeply into your psyche and soul, picked apart your life and your brain, I am ready to make my recommendation to the rest of your family and friends. My analysis of you shows clearly that you are an adult child of an alcoholic, a flaming co-dependent, Al-Anon, overeating, controlling, manipulative person with tendencies to shame, blame, demean, demoralize, criticize, preach, teach and judge. Now, don't get me wrong—I'm not angry with you—I'm just trying to figure you out. I've looked at your mother and studied your father carefully, and I think I am ready to write up my diagnosis and 'share' with you my prognosis. But as your analyst—I mean daughter—who brings nothing but objectivity to you, my client—I mean my father—it is my professional opinion that you should go to ninety meetings in ninety days, read the Big Book every day, take Zoloft in the mornings and Wellbutrin in the evenings, go to church on Sundays, meditate, and pay me two hundred and fifty dollars an hour for being your therapist—I mean child. As your therapist—

I mean son—I am now going to explain to you in a way even you can understand—just kidding."

After all of this someone is going to need a drink.

Still unsure if any of this applies? Listed below are a number of telltale signs that we are filled with rage.

Rigidity

Rage takes the form of a rigid body and rigid thinking. Rigid folks fear flexibility because flexible people feel.

All-or-Nothing Attitude

This is the old "my way or the highway" form of rage. "Either go and see a counselor or we're through," said Joseph to his wife. He felt he knew the "only way for her to be helped" was to do what he said.

Black-and-White Thinking

An extreme point of view is a form of rage. "You're wrong and I'm right." "All Muslims are terrorists." "Dad was a mean drunk, mother was a saint."

Verbal Threats

"If you don't go to AA I'm leaving you." "If you leave now I won't be here when you return." "Go to bed and get to sleep before I come in there—and you don't want me to come in there." "Stop crying or I'll give you something to cry about."

Word Games

"You call me critical, but I'm just concerned for your happiness." "I didn't say that exactly."

We've all heard these things so often. We've seen these behaviors displayed in some way by our loved ones, and we've engaged in them too—so often that we've come to think this is just the way it is. But if our bodies are not numbed or severely medicated, all of these forms of rage leave us feeling yucky at best and devastated at worst.

THE DIFFERENCE BETWEEN
RAGE AND ANGER

Unfortunately, many of us, and I include myself, use certain words interchangeably just as if they meant the same thing. Many say self-pity when they mean grief. Others confuse sympathy and empathy, which I'll say much more about later. But the words "anger" and "rage" are constantly spoken in the same sentence by therapists, counselors and the general public, educated and noneducated alike. They do not mean the same thing. Anger is a feeling, as stated earlier, that comes, goes, and doesn't do any damage to the body or the soul. It is an emotion that moves in, through and out of the body and can usually be expressed quickly. Rage on the other hand is not—I repeat, is *not*—a feeling, but an **action** or **behavior** that is used to numb our feelings and medicate our emotions temporarily. Rage is just as effective in numbing our feelings of sadness, fear, loneliness and, yes, even anger, as any drug, narcotic, stimulant, alcohol, food bingeing and purging, sex addiction or workaholism.

When I am shaming, blaming or demeaning you, I am raging at you. I am not feeling anything. When I am demoralizing, criticizing, preaching at you, trying to teach, judging you or analyzing you, I am not telling you how I feel. I am not opening my inner, emotional self to you. I am in my head, not feeling a thing, but unconsciously wanting you to feel terrible about what you said or did, didn't say or didn't do that scared me, hurt me, made me sad or made me angry. Now the politically correct among my readers are saying to themselves, "No one can make you anything." And perhaps you are right. But bear with me a few more moments.

Likewise, when I am interrogating, intimidating, distancing myself from you or playing the poor-me, I am using behaviors and taking actions to make my feelings go away temporarily—just as drinking alcohol or ingesting a drug will do.

Here is a list of other behaviors and actions that are examples of rage, not anger:

1. Being chronically late for appointments, meetings, dates
2. Controlling others
3. Manipulating others
4. Withholding sex
5. Not telephoning someone back but keeping them guessing
6. Engaging in put-downs
7. Practicing one-upmanship
8. Telling cruel jokes
9. Making racist comments

10. Engaging in gay bashing
11. Making sexist comments

So, when my clients or workshop participants tell me their husbands, wives or parents are very angry or so angry, what they really mean to say is that they are raging. Some examples: My ex-love's father was not an angry young man: He was a man full of rage, and he behaved and acted like a man full of rage. He made many sexist, racist and gay-bashing statements. When a mother beats her children with her hairbrush, she is not angry, she is enraged. She is acting, behaving and not feeling because if she were truly feeling her feelings she would also feel in her body that she must not hit her child. Dennis Rodman, the basketball player, is not angry. Mike Tyson, the boxer who bit off Evander Holyfield's ear, is not angry. Both are full of rage, and this rage keeps all our feelings at bay.

HOW TO TELL THE DIFFERENCE
BETWEEN ANGER AND RAGE

There are a number of ways to tell the differences between rage and anger. Rage takes a long time to express—hours, days, weeks, months, years and lifetimes. Anger expressed appropriately takes minutes at the most. Rage is never resolved in a short conversation. Anger is done in a sentence or two, perhaps three or four. Rage consists of paragraphs, pages, volumes and epics. With rage there is no relief when expressed. Anger expressed relaxes us and sometimes even the other person because now they feel safer with us because they know how we feel. Rage always equals distance, disaster and divorce. Anger equals closeness, order and clearer communication. When men or women or children rage everyone feels tired and drained. When we express anger we usually feel refreshed and rejuvenated. Rage tends to hurt everyone in the near vicinity of it and anger tends to hurt no one—not even the dead, much less the living. Let me be a little repetitive here and say again that rage is an action or a behavior used to numb our feelings, and anger is just a feeling, neither positive nor negative, and hurts no one any more than expressing sadness or joy does.

WHY DO WE RAGE?

The short answer to this question is that most of us have never seen anger expressed appropriately. We only know how to do what someone, somewhere, sometime showed us. As children we see an intimidator go up against a poor pitiful me and unconsciously we pick the one behavior that looks better to us. Having seen these behaviors modeled year after year, we are certain that everyone does anger this way and there are no other ways. There is no person on Earth who at thirteen decided to withdraw and distance him- or herself from everyone as if they had created this behavior and it was unique to them. While they may not have seen their parents demonstrate this action to them, you can bet they saw it somewhere. No child ever decides one day, at eight or nine, "Hey, I think I'll invent being a raging, lunatic drug addict and be that way until I'm sixty-five years old and am divorced four times."

Rage is easy, takes no thought and concerns itself with no one. "Flying off the handle," "Straightening someone's ass out," "Setting them straight," "Calling them on their bullshit" or "Cursing them out" is what was done to us. And it is what we do to our friends, children, employees, husbands and wives—all under the rationale that they need us to do this for them or that we're just "telling it like it is," "being rigorously honest," or "telling our truth as we see it."

Listed below are some other reasons we rage.

- Alcoholics/addicts and the people who love us are angry at the diseases but don't know what to do about them, and so feel helpless, impotent and out of control.
- Alcoholics/addicts hate the very stuff we put in our bodies, and we hate ourselves for putting it in our bodies. Those who love alcoholics and addicts hate the same stuff.
- Alcoholics/addicts have been searching for God all their lives, think he/she/it has abandoned them and question if he/she/it ever existed in the first place.
- Alcoholics/addicts and the people who love them are scared to death of the unknown and sometimes stay with people and in places longer than they should.
- 99.9 percent of all alcoholics/addicts were physically, emotionally or spiritually abused—or all three—and so were most of the people who live with or marry us, or else they would have found someone healthy.
- People who love or live with us have been abused as well and misconstrue abuse and abandonment for love.
- 50 percent of all adult children of alcoholics/addicts will

become alcoholics/addicts, and the other fifty percent will marry one.

- Ninety-nine and five-tenths of all alcoholics/addicts were punished rather than disciplined as children.

HOW DO WE GO FROM RAGE TO ANGER?

First, we have to separate one from the other and not keep thinking anger and rage are the same things. We have to become conscious of our rage in order to get to our anger. We have to find safe ways to reduce our rage, which then allows us to get not only to our anger but also to our grief and sadness, and eventually our joy. This is known as "rage reduction work," and it scares the hell out of most people, not to mention many well-intentioned therapists and counselors who have not come out of denial about their own rage, and who consciously reduced it themselves—usually with the help of another therapist or therapy group.

The more we reduce our pent-up, past rage the more we can feel. The more we can feel the less we will tolerate someone raging at us because it won't "feel good" or "right."

Remember, anger . . .
- takes only a few minutes to express
- doesn't hurt anyone, including yourself
- doesn't drain your energy
- creates intimacy
- makes everyone feel better in the long run

- is what adults and children do before they are shut down
- is a God-given emotion
- is neither positive nor negative
- is a primary emotion
- leaves you with a feeling of release and relaxation.

3

THE SOLUTION— THE BEGINNING

REDUCING ANGER AT OURSELVES FIRST

AT MY ANGER INTENSIVES and lectures on the subject, I ask participants with whom they are angry. Ninety-nine people out of one hundred—*all* one hundred if they are alcoholics or addicts—say "Me!" They are angry with themselves. I ask them to try and see that if they have that much anger at themselves is it any wonder that they punish themselves, abuse themselves, abandon themselves and see themselves as low as the stuff under their refrigerators? Men and women who are convinced they should be angry with themselves are like waterwheels that keep dipping into the same turbulent water, pulling it up and letting it drop back into the same pool. Or they are like fountains: the anger shoots up and then falls right back down into their bodies where they recycle it repeatedly. Every so often they have to take a drink, a drug, a process or a person into themselves to temporarily numb the pain of this repetitive compulsion.

Anger should be seen and experienced like a waterfall instead of a waterwheel. The anger should come out of us and drop off into the riverbed to be absorbed and sent downstream where the ocean embraces it without affecting it in any negative way. In other words, anger should come up and go out away from the body, leaving the body and the brain a little emptier so that there is room for reasonable thoughts and the constant stream of emotions. Anger that comes up and goes back into our bodies results in the same feelings we experienced when our parents, teachers, principals or coaches hurled their anger into our tender young bodies—it hurts us.

Just yesterday, I was working with a woman who "never finishes anything," and when we went back into her past, one of the first memories she had was loving to swim competitively at six years old but having to practice in an unheated pool in the wintertime. She told the coach it was too cold and he pushed her small body in anyway. She quit swimming that day and convinced herself that she was "angry at myself for never finishing anything. Now I realize I am angry at him and have been for years, but I always repressed it until now." The poet Rainer Maria Rilke says, "The abused becomes the abuser." We abuse others and ourselves, repeating what was done to us.

Next up is a discussion about one of the worst things ever done to us and how we embraced it as something that is right, true and even healthy. If we can come to terms with the following we will radically lessen our anger and rage.

READER/CUSTOMER CARE SURVEY

We care about your opinions! Please take a moment to fill out our online Reader Survey at **http://survey.hcibooks.com.**
As a **"THANK YOU"** you will receive a **VALUABLE INSTANT COUPON** towards future book purchases as well as a **SPECIAL GIFT** available only online! Or, you may mail this card back to us and we will send you a copy of our exciting catalog with your valuable coupon inside.

(PLEASE PRINT IN ALL CAPS)

First Name		MI.		Last Name	

Address				City	

State		Zip		Email	

1. Gender
☐ Female   ☐ Male

2. Age
☐ 8 or younger
☐ 9-12   ☐ 13-16
☐ 17-20   ☐ 21-30
☐ 31+

3. Did you receive this book as a gift?
☐ Yes   ☐ No

4. Annual Household Income
☐ under $25,000
☐ $25,000 - $34,999
☐ $35,000 - $49,999
☐ $50,000 - $74,999
☐ over $75,000

5. What are the ages of the children living in your house?
☐ 0 - 14   ☐ 15+

6. Marital Status
☐ Single
☐ Married
☐ Divorced
☐ Widowed

7. How did you find out about the book?
(please choose one)
☐ Recommendation
☐ Store Display
☐ Online
☐ Catalog/Mailing
☐ Interview/Review

8. Where do you usually buy books?
(please choose one)
☐ Bookstore
☐ Online
☐ Book Club/Mail Order
☐ Price Club (Sam's Club, Costco's, etc.)
☐ Retail Store (Target, Wal-Mart, etc.)

9. What subject do you enjoy reading about the most?
(please choose one)
☐ Parenting/Family
☐ Relationships
☐ Recovery/Addictions
☐ Health/Nutrition
☐ Christianity
☐ Spirituality/Inspiration
☐ Business Self-help
☐ Women's Issues
☐ Sports

10. What attracts you most to a book?
(please choose one)
☐ Title
☐ Cover Design
☐ Author
☐ Content

TAPE IN MIDDLE; DO NOT STAPLE

BUSINESS REPLY MAIL
FIRST-CLASS MAIL PERMIT NO 45 DEERFIELD BEACH, FL

POSTAGE WILL BE PAID BY ADDRESSEE

Health Communications, Inc.
3201 SW 15th Street
Deerfield Beach FL 33442-9875

FOLD HERE

Comments

ASSIGNING ACCOUNTABILITY AND
TAKING RESPONSIBILITY

Earlier I said people tend to confuse words and use them interchangeably. "Accountability" and "responsibility" are good examples. Unfortunately, many well-intentioned therapists, priests and sponsors misunderstand these two incredibly powerful and potent words, telling their listeners that they are accountable when they should say responsible and responsible when they mean accountable. Webster defines accountability as "liable to pay or make good in case of loss." Responsibility, says the dictionary, is being "able to respond to any claim."

Let me give an example. If I am driving down the road at the speed limit, and I come to an intersection and see the light is green and proceed through the intersection, and then a car zoom-zooms through its red light and runs into me and my car—who is accountable? The red-light runner—that's who. I'm going to get out of my car, shaken up a bit, probably a little scared and probably a little angry if I'm not too much in shock (which I'll say much more about later), and I'm going to ask the man or woman if he or she has insurance to pay for my damaged car and "make good in case of loss." I will hold the other driver "accountable" and then I'll be "responsible" and take my car to the body shop to have it repaired.

If I hold myself accountable for someone running the red light, I am telling myself that it was my fault for being in the wrong place at the wrong time and telling the red-light runner, "Oh, I'm so sorry I got in your line of fire. How silly of me to think I could drive down the road expecting others to obey the law. It's not necessary to contact your insurance agent. I'll pay for the damages—yours and mine. Have a good day." Just as equally ridiculous as this would be saying something like, "Look, you red-light runner you, come by my house tomorrow and pick up my damaged car and take it to the body shop and go back and pick it up when they are done and bring it to me and in the meantime give me the keys to your wife's car, which I'll be driving until you get mine fixed." The bottom line is: you ran into me, so you are accountable. I'll take the car to be fixed—I'm responsible for getting the repairs done.

Another way to think about this is that if you carry both the weight of accountability and the weight of responsibility, the two weights together will weigh you down so much you'll be exhausted and probably not have enough strength to handle either. You'll probably drink, drug or get very depressed. Most of the men and women I have worked with, and I include myself in this, thought when we were children that we were the reasons why our father or mother drank, drugged or beat us. (I've heard hundreds say, "I probably deserved it. I was always getting into some kind of trouble.") We make ourselves accountable and responsible for their behavior. Even if we were ignored, left or smothered, we assigned ourselves accountability right from childhood on.

My father's life ran into my life when I was young, and he wrecked it with his alcohol, abuse and abandonment. If I get angry at myself for this, I'll never heal, never trust other men, and I'll perpetuate the same behavior in my children. By getting angry at what I call "the ghost father"—not the one living today down in Florida, but the one who was maybe too young to drive/be a father—I can then carry the right weight of responsibility and go take my wrecked body/life to the body shop/therapist/recovery and get it fixed. And since my dad didn't take out faulty father insurance, I'll have to be responsible for coming up with the money to have the work done.

What I did and still do—and suggest that my clients and workshop participants do—is assign accountability and take responsibility. Most of the time this is never done face to face but in the form of writing letters that we do not send, fantasy dialoguing, sharing with a therapist, storytelling, creating and other means.

I recall the time I was wrestling with why I treated the one I loved so much less than kindly when I visited my parents. (See my first book, *The Flying Boy: Healing the Wounded Man*, Health Communications, Inc.). Twenty years ago, I was sitting in Dad's La-Z-Boy, talking to him and my mother, and a knock came on the door. My dad got up and went to the door. It was the electrician he called to fix some electrical problem they were having.

"How you doin', neighbor," he said. "So glad to meet you, and I can't thank you enough for coming out on a weekend. Let me show you the way to the switch box. If there's anything I can do to be of help, just give me a yell."

Then my dad came back into the living room where Mom was lying on the couch and said in a cruel tone of voice, but in a whisper, "Get up off your lazy ass, woman, and get that man something cool to drink." I burst into tears and started saying, "You, you, you . . ."

Dad said, "Now just calm down and tell me what's wrong. 'You' what?"

Through the tears and sobbing I got out, "You, you are the one who taught me this. You taught me how to treat women like crap. You have treated this woman who has gone through hell and back with you like crap. You talk to the electrician, who you have never met before, like he was a king and you treat Mom like a slave. I learned this from you. For thirty years I thought I invented this behavior. I just watched you. Well, it's going to stop here and now. I'm going to get all the help I need from wherever I have to so I'll stop treating strangers like royalty and lovers like garbage. No matter how much therapy or how many self-help books I have to read—it stops here."

"Okay Son, just calm down. Your mother knows I love her."

Here is another example of holding someone accountable so you won't think I'm just parent bashing or blaming. When I went to college at seventeen, it didn't take me long to realize I had not been prepared for college level work. I remember thinking back then that I was stupid, dumb, ignorant and illiterate. I was angry with myself for being this way. It took me a long time to shake those labels. Looking back, I had a slightly above average IQ, but the school I went to in Alabama was way below the national average in literacy. Even to this day Alabama and Mississippi are always arguing over the title of poorest educational facilities.

I turned my anger inward for a long time before I realized through much hard work that the schools and teachers were accountable to teach and I was responsible to learn. While there were a few good teachers, there were many more who "pushed" many of us from grade to grade to get rid of us and make room for others coming behind us. Also, my experience was that school was more like a day-care center for us career juvenile delinquents who smashed more than a few street lamps and smoked behind the gym. Finally, I felt my anger with the educational system that rolled me out on its conveyor belt before it tightened all my bolts and double-checked my intellectual and scholastic engine. Then I had to become responsible for doing something about this, which in my case meant learning stuff I should have learned in junior and senior high school. I had to study three times as hard as my fellow students who lived in school districts that held their teachers accountable for teaching the proper information and dispensing a reasonable education.

I've worked with many people who are angry with themselves for so many things. They don't know how to pray, and they hold themselves accountable instead of the ministers, preachers and teachers whose job it is to teach them how to pray. There are those who are angry with themselves for being fifty years old and not knowing "how to do a relationship," as if they were supposed to be born with this info. We do, we repeat, we parrot what was shown to us, what was taught to us—until we get out from under the weight of holding ourselves accountable. We get angry, get sad and then get responsible for educating ourselves about prayer, relationships, childrearing, learning how to love, being intimate, making love instead of lust and so on.

THE DIFFERENCE BETWEEN ACCOUNTABILITY AND BLAMING

Every time alcoholics fill their glass with poison they are blaming someone or something for their condition. Every time an addict sticks something in his mouth, nose or arm he is demonstrating his pain, but also his self-pity and blame for the way life has or has not treated him.

Every time an adult child of an alcoholic keeps repeating dysfunctional patterns in relationships—getting in them too quickly, getting out of them twenty years after they should have—she is blaming and raging, and therefore she is drained and exhausted. Blame creates distance, it hurts everyone and nothing is accomplished at all. Writing a letter of accountability hurts no one. Telling your sponsor how your father beat you and taught you to beat your son is more likely to motivate you to stop abusing your children. Admitting to your therapist that your parents, schools, churches or synagogues taught you little or nothing about how to have mature relationships humbles you enough to take responsibility to learn. Getting angry with who or what is accountable gets people out of stuck places and into the flow of a healthy life. And nothing will help a person stay in the flow of life like understanding regression—what it is, what the signs and feelings are, and how to catch it so we do less damage to ourselves and the ones we like, love, work or deal with.

Without a thorough understanding of regression, expressing anger appropriately is almost impossible. By exploring and working with regression, what I call the "best-kept secret in psychology," we rage less, enjoy life more, and thus drink and drug less. And ultimately, we have more peace in our lives.

4

UNDERSTANDING EMOTIONAL REGRESSION

REGRESSION

WHAT EXACTLY IS REGRESSION? In layperson's terms it is our tendency to return to our past—an unexpected, unintentional revisiting of our history. And while we are doing so, we feel small and very much like a child in an adult's body, as powerless as we were as children. We go from the chronological age we actually are to acting, thinking, behaving, speaking or withholding like teenagers, children and infants. (Note: Not all regression entails going back to childhood. A forty-year-old can act like a twenty-year-old. I'll discuss this more in detail later.) One minute we are fifty with mortgages and credit cards and the next minute we want our blanket and bottle. For alcoholics and addicts, the blanket may be the drugs that we crawl under while we wait for the bad, uncomfortable things to stop happening, and the bottle is the whisky, vodka or gin bottle instead of mother's milk or the milk of human kindness, both of which are sorely lacking in many people's past and present. After all, all alcoholics and addicts are starving and thirsty for something they cannot name.

HOW REGRESSION RELATES TO RAGE

When we experience what should make us feel angry or sad, we tend to return to our histories and react the way someone modeled for us in our past. If during a situation we start feeling little, we pick one of the forms of rage—shaming, blaming, withholding, demeaning, interrogating—because that is all we know how to do. Regressed men and women rage; adults express anger once they come back into the present.

WHAT MAKES US REGRESS?

Different things make different people return to childhood and feel little or small. What makes one person regress may not affect another person at all. So many things incite regression that they are too numerous to list, but I'll give you the main ones and you can then make your own list.

- Certain sounds: police or fire trucks, slammed door, heavy footsteps.
- Certain looks: a cold stare, faraway look, raised eyebrow.
- Tones of voice: gruff, whiny, yelling.

- Gestures: a pointed finger, shoulder shrug, the middle finger.
- Postures: hands on the hips, being looked down upon, someone standing too close.
- Words: "I'm out of here." "I hate you." "It's all good." "Go to hell."
- Being left alone: after a divorce, during an illness, when the children leave home, when a loved one moves away.
- Being smothered: too much attention, having no privacy, having someone else make decisions for you.

Generally, regression happens when there is **too much** or **too little** of something. Too much noise, and some regress. Too little sound, and people feel small. Too much food or too little. Too much sex or not enough. Too much touch or too little, causing touch starvation. Too little money and, yes, too much. If you look at the history of those who win the lottery, most of them spend like children and end up broke.

Regression also tends to occur when we are tired, sick, hungry, isolated, overworked and most of all stressed. These conditions usually guarantee regression and then we act out in a variety of ways, from extreme neediness to an attitude of "leave me alone," from rage to being totally shut down.

Purchasing large-ticket items will make most of us regress. Buying a car or home can be a catalyst for regression. Edward told me about the time he and his wife were looking for a home to buy. He wanted an old Victorian fixer-upper and she wanted a brand new home in Chicago's most posh new suburb. Every time they would go out looking at homes both of them would regress. "One Sunday," Edward said, "we looked all day, and by the time we went back to our apartment, about all I could say was 'Me want house, me want big house to play in, me no care how much it costs. Mommy and Daddy buy me a big house.'" We both had a good laugh because I could relate with his situation.

HOW TO KNOW WHEN YOU ARE REGRESSED

Here is an incomplete list of ways you can know you are regressing. (For more in-depth information on regression see my book *Growing Yourself Back Up: Understanding Emotional Regression*, Three Rivers Press, 2001.)

Physical Signs and Symptoms of Regression

- Cold, clammy, or sweaty hands
- Cold feet
- Dry mouth
- Sweating profusely
- Rapid heartbeat
- Shallow breathing
- Extreme physical gesturing
- Knot in stomach
- Very tense shoulders or back

Psychological and Emotional Signs of Regression

- You feel like you don't have a choice. (Adults almost always have a choice; as children we did not.)
- Time moves faster than the speed of light.

- Time seems to stand still.
- We create elaborate stories in our minds about situations or people.
- Black-and-white thinking and speaking; all-or-nothing thinking and speaking.
- We are shut down to all feelings.
- We think we know what others need without asking them.
- We are afraid to ask for help.
- We drink a quart of vodka every night.
- We eat a gallon of ice cream.
- We shoot poison into our bodies.
- We stay in abusive relationships.

When people experience any of the above there is a likelihood of rage. Rage is what men and women do when they are regressed. They return to their histories, and then out come all the things they wished they had said thirty or forty years ago but could not, or all the things they wanted to do but could not—like leave.

A client we'll call Martha left her second husband and moved into her own apartment and lived there for three years. She attended an emotional regression workshop and didn't think she got much out of it until the last thing I said that afternoon: "Be sure not to push the wrong person out the door." A week later she moved back in with her husband after coming out of a regression she had been in most of her life.

"I always wanted to leave my father's house and my ex-husband's long before I did," Martha explained. "I was pushing the wrong person out of my life and leaving a husband who I really do love."

We have been storing these desires in our body/mind for decades. We do the things that we wish we could have done earlier, but didn't do because we might have been physically or emotionally hurt.

Burt's father, who was an alcoholic during Burt's entire childhood, was always late picking him up from school, if he showed up at all. Burt would wait sometimes an hour or two before walking a mile home, which for a six-year-old is quite a journey. So when anyone runs even five or ten minutes late for lunch, or an appointment, he begins to tell himself stories like, "They don't care about me," "They're not coming," "I'm not important to them," and then when they finally do show up, he blasts them with loud silence or sometimes with verbal harangues. But his reactions are always disproportional to the event. For Burt, keeping him waiting opens a small window of opportunity through which he pushes out ten thousand pounds of rage and hurt. Burt says what he wishes he could have said to his chronically late father. His reaction is out of proportion to the event that is happening in present time. This is a huge red flag of regression. His wife, who never intentionally keeps him waiting, has told him on more than several occasions that he is overreacting and asks, "Where is all of this rage coming from?" Until he worked with his history a few times, he could truthfully say he really didn't know; he thought that it was really about what was happening in the present.

When we are not regressed, things and people still make us angry but we respond instead of react, and our response is proportional to the situation or circumstances. Adults respond; regressed men and women react. Adults express their frustration, disappointment, anger and hurt in a few minutes and then move on. Regression takes much longer and is usually about us and our histories. Most people in the present are left confused by our behavior because even our closest friends, spouses or lovers don't completely know our history. How could they? We don't even remember most of our histories until something is said or not said, done or not done that restimulates memories that have been buried in the graveyard of our bodies.

ADDING ALCOHOL AND DRUGS TO REGRESSION

Many years ago when I was on the road constantly, lecturing and giving workshops, I got so exhausted I entered a recurring state of regression. Sometimes at two A.M. I would cry like a baby. I wanted to be home with my family but was so fearful of our economic insecurity. My dad went bankrupt when I was sixteen, and my new car was repossessed after I had it for only a month. I vowed I would never go bankrupt, be without money, and be that embarrassed and hurt again. I kept pushing myself, not knowing my limits, and ended up relapsing for a short period and turning once again to alcohol to numb the pain, the fear and the loneliness. And guess what? I had to declare bankruptcy just like my father did forty years before.

How regressed must we be when we think taking several drinks or drugs will help the situation? The answer is pretty damned regressed. How regressed must one be to do what Martha—who has been in recovery for seventeen years from alcohol and drugs—did, which was take abuse from her boyfriend, who is a chronic relapser and prone to violence? How regressed must Barbara be when she opens the door to the freezer and eats a gallon of Häagen-Dazs ice cream? And then how regressed is she afterward?

WHAT ARE WE REALLY HUNGRY FOR WHEN WE'RE REGRESSED?

When we regress we tend to return to those things that comforted us once upon a time, or we return to what we saw comforted those we loved or lived with, or both. For many of us the first comforter was sugar. For example, my mother would give us white Wonder Bread with butter and lots of sugar. When we feel low we look for comfort food, which is usually filled with sugar. One of the main ingredients of most alcoholic drinks is a vast quantity of sugar. My mother took sedatives. My father shot up work and drowned his blues in White Lightning. Guess which ones I used? All of the above.

What my parents needed was someone to pay attention to them during the times of distress. You might recall in the wonderful play *Death of a Salesman* that Willie Loman's wife cries out at the end, "Attention, attention must be paid to this man," who was in a terminal state of regression, which is suicide. The problem with the number-one thing we need when we are regressed—attention—is that very few of us have been taught to really pay attention to ourselves or to ask for or receive support. What we were taught was to ignore our need for attention for fear of sounding or looking pitiful or weak. When most people see someone who is regressed, they try to "fix," "recommend to" or "take care of" them. But they do not pay undivided attention to someone who is hurting, scared, angry, and feeling small and less than powerful. Trying to fix another adult, giving unsolicited advice and taking care of him as if he were an infant actually regresses the person further and makes him feel even more like a child. And this tends to generate anger/rage.

The other problem with attention is that most of us don't know how to receive it gracefully. We feel awkward when someone wants to really pay attention to us, or we may feel undeserving of his or her time or believe that someone else needs it more than we do. I can't count the number of men and women who have sat down beside me in my workshops to try to heal some traumas and who began sobbing and weeping uncontrollably. After several minutes of this, they often would say, "No one has ever just paid attention to me like this, and I'm fifty, sixty or seventy years old."

Good, clear, loving attention will help just about anyone grow themselves up out of their histories and return them to their present adult state. Poor or no attention will regress the person further. They will usually get enraged that there is no one to whom they can turn and get the attention they need. So they act out—drinking, drugging, engaging in addictive behaviors, becoming ill or doing whatever they have to do— to get that negative attention that is better than none. A child will pull a lamp off the table and risk a whipping because it is better than being ignored.

WHAT ATTENTION LOOKS
AND SOUNDS LIKE

Attention is quietly given. You hear the attention-giver's breathing, because if the regressed person doesn't hear it she will subconsciously know that the person who is trying to be there for her can't be or he is regressing himself. Those who can provide good attention will gently look at you, not bore a hole into you, but look at you with soft, gentle eyes. Occasionally the attention-giver nods his head up and down to show understanding and nonjudgment. His body says: "I am here. Say everything you need to say. Feel everything you need to. Bring all your unwanted parts to the process because your warts and all do not scare me or turn me off in any way. I'm here."

Giving and Receiving Empathy

When someone is feeling small, the last thing she needs is sympathy. The dictionary defines sympathy as "feeling what another person feels." If I am in my full adult state I don't want to feel anyone's feelings but my own, and I want to honor all other adults by supporting them to do the same. Should I slip into my own regression, I take on your feelings as if you cannot handle them on your own, which regresses you even more by effectively saying, "You're not strong enough and I am."

Empathy means, "I understand some of what you are going through because I have been through similar experiences myself." Empathy says, "I am me and have my feelings and you are you and have your feelings, but let's get through this thing—whatever it is that is causing you to regress—the best way we can."

Unfortunately, many laypeople and therapists confuse the two words—sympathy and empathy—and many use them interchangeably. Also, many have been taught that the only way to be a truly loving person is to sympathize with others and say what former President Bill Clinton once said to the public: "I feel your pain." Even when I'm regressed I don't want you to feel my pain. But I do want you to understand some of it, listen to it, and see me be in it until I can come out of it.

When we were children we very much wanted someone to feel the pain we were in. You are supposed to feel your small children's pains and discomforts, but not your seventeen-year-old's. If you do they will have to pull away even further to show you that they are separate from you. It is necessary to feel the aged and infirmed person's pain if they are not cognizant due to some incapacitation such as Alzheimer's or other mental defects. If adults sympathize with an elderly person who is completely lucid and coherent it will make them very angry at best. They may want you to go away and stay away at worst, because they do not want to be treated as children.

Attention and empathy go hand in hand. Together they are the ladders out of our histories on which we can climb free of the past and up to the present. This is one reason why the Twelve-Step programs work so well. However, reader, be advised that there are healthy meetings and not so healthy ones all over the country. (Note: "Old-timers" are fond of saying, "There are no bad meetings.") At good meetings you get to speak and "put out on the table" what is disturbing you or threatening your sobriety, and most of the people in the room will pay attention and empathize with you.

Time

Time is the third component that will grow up a regressed person. Sometimes we just need to take some time to ourselves and be alone to come out of our histories. We may need to take a long walk or a drive in the country or sit quietly in a peaceful spot. The poet Wallace Stevens said, "Sometimes, the truth depends on a walk around the lake." I can recall many times I wish I had taken that walk instead of saying or doing what I did to someone I loved while in a regression.

The downside is that most people feel like they don't have time in their busy day to take a time-out, and so they plunge headfirst into an argument, discussion or problem while they are regressed. They do this only to discover that it wastes much more time than it would have taken to pull away temporarily and grow themselves back up through attention, empathy and time.

Sometimes I can grow myself up by taking some alone time. Other times I need another person or two to give me a little of their time to get me centered in the present moment.

Contact

When men and women are in a regressed state, most feel alone. That can be very scary for anyone who is feeling like a two-year-old. Sometimes what is most needed is someone to spend time with you and give you attention and empathy. You need contact with someone who is not regressed, who can maintain his adultness while seeing and experiencing the regressed person who is drowning in the deep waters of her past. This contact can be made over the phone, eye to eye, or with a hand on the shoulder. (Note: I always ask if this is all right because touching someone without his or her permission may cause regression even further into a history of unwanted touch or unsafe touch.) I will often hold out my hand for a person to take if she feels it is right and useful. Contact lets the person know she is not alone in this battle with her demons or her difficulties. Sadly, when people are regressed they tend to exacerbate it by isolating and not reaching out, and often the result is maximized regression.

Unfortunately, when we are regressed we forget to ask others for their time. In our regression we may feel embarrassed, ashamed and unworthy of anyone's time, especially if we have asked them for it in the past around the same regressive issue.

It is best if we have at least four or five people who make up a strong net that we can fall into when we slip into our past. Sometimes one or another of these people may be regressed and unable to give us attention, time or contact. But if we have several people, we can usually find one or two who are in an adult state.

Emotional Release

The last, but certainly not the least, of the things that will help the regressed man or woman return to the here and now is emotional release. When you are regressed there is always a tendency to tense up, contract, pull in, tighten up, cover the tender spots and generally shrink. Emotional release, whether it's crying, shouting, writing in your journal, sobbing, talking, laughing, pounding, twisting or simply letting out a deep sigh or full, deep breath, will allow for expansion, relaxation, rejuvenation and generally opening back up in direct proportion to how safe the regressed person feels.

What alcoholics and addicts do is take in outside things to make them forget they haven't gotten attention, empathy, time, contact and especially emotional release—given that their emotions are numbed. Instead of releasing their feelings they numb them and further regress—contracting, pulling away, isolating and feeling abandoned—and the result is anger that doesn't get felt but acted out through the rageful ways I discussed earlier.

HOW TO KNOW IF YOU'RE
OUT OF YOUR REGRESSION

- You are now able to take full deep breaths.
- Time is back to normal, that is, a week seems like a week, a day seems like a day, a month seems like a month.
- Your body is back to a state of equilibrium and balance.
- You think like a mature adult.
- You talk like a mature adult.
- You become more compassionate with other men and women who regress just as you do.
- You express your feelings appropriately.
- You don't minimize or dramatize situations.
- You say what you think.
- Your response is proportional to the situation.
- You ask for what you really need.
- You set boundaries and defend them.

- You know your limits and don't go past them unless you change your mind by getting new or more information.

HELPING OTHERS WHEN THEY REGRESS

It is very important to remember that if someone is regressed and calls upon you to help grow him back up that you do so because you genuinely feel capable, and that you do not do it because of your inability to say no. He will sense this incongruity and will regress even further. Also, if what is regressing him triggers your own issues, be honest and tell him so that he can go somewhere else to get what he needs. Otherwise, you will regress and be angry with yourself for not setting good boundaries.

Good people still do so much damage when they are regressed, not to mention people who are high, drunk or stoned. So many things are said and done that can never be taken back or ever made right. Men and women make huge, life-changing decisions while feeling like a four-year-old. If this sounds like regression is a bad thing and that we are bad people for doing it, let me be clear: Regression is part of the human condition. It is not a neurosis or psychosis; it is not abnormal behavior. Indeed, people would be abnormal if they didn't regress from time to time. Regression can't be cured, but it can be curtailed and caught sooner than later in direct proportion to how much the regressive process is understood. Then there will be less physical, emotional and spiritual damage done to those you love, live with, work for or play with.

Making use of the Detour Method, the subject of the next chapter, is one of the most useful tools I know to minimize miscommunication, misunderstanding and anger among everyone concerned.

5

THE DETOUR METHOD

I've taught thousands of people in several countries how to effectively use the simple, yet elegant tool that I call the Detour Method™. I've been learning, using and teaching this process to cope with anger, rage, fear, resentment and other emotions for twenty years.

Twenty years ago, when it came time to doing day- or weeklong workshops, I did most of them by myself. (As a kid in an alcoholic/addict family, I did quite a bit alone and was afraid to ask for help—a common problem for alcoholics and addicts.) Inevitably, before the workshop was over I'd say something, *not* say something, do something or *not* do something that would trigger someone's memories of their painful or traumatic past. Then, during or after a workshop, I'd be exhausted and someone would come up to me and say something like, "We need to talk"—which means *they* need to, whether it is a good time or not, whether there are twenty-five people in the other room or not. "We need to talk" is a phrase filled with regression and usually rage about something I said or didn't say that triggered in them a huge reaction. It's a phrase that, when said, is still more painful than poking a sharp stick in my eye. They would talk and I'd listen. They would proceed to attempt to work out their history with me, as if I were the perpetrator of some hurtful event or cruel thing said or done years before. Sometimes this "working out" would take an hour; I'd be further drained and they would be no further satisfied. Remember that rage can take hours, days or forever to work through, with no satisfactory resolution.

The first time I really saw this was when I was leading a men's gathering in Texas. There were one hundred and fifty men attending the weekend event. On the second day a young man came up to me and said, "We've got to talk. I have been here two days and you have yet to make eye contact with me and I want to know why." He looked very angry and very sad at the same time. I really didn't know much about regression at the time.

"Who are you?" I asked him. "You don't know me, do you?"

"No, I really don't."

A few tears fell from his eyes and I could see a light go off behind them.

"I did it again," he said. "I made you into my father. He never saw me. He could never look me in the eyes, and I always wanted him to see me more than anything. I loved him so much." Now tears were really streaming down his face.

Right then I realized that I'd done the very same thing many times before—made a person into someone other than who he or she was. I didn't see them. I made many women into my mom. I made some of them into my dad. I made others into my high school sweetheart, who hurt me to the core. All of them just wanted to be seen for who they really were. I saw them through the filter of my history and my regression, and this made many of them justifiably angry and sad. Many of them made me into fathers and mothers and ex-lovers that I'd never met, and this made me angry and hurt as well.

Shortly after this event I had a TMM (a temporary moment of maturity) and decided from then on I'd train people to assist me at all my longer events. With the help of my Higher Power and Dan Jones, my good friend and colleague, we came up with the process I now call the Detour Method.

WHAT IS THE DETOUR METHOD?

At the beginning of each workshop, I now tell the folks attending that if I say something, don't say something, do something or don't do something that triggers a huge reaction in them, to please ask one of my assistants to go with them to process what just came up. If they are so angry with me that they feel like walking out of the seminar at best, or going for my throat at worst, then the Detour Method is highly encouraged.

When the way you want to go is blocked, you are forced to

take a detour. Regression and remembering our history make up that block. Instead of going directly to the person with whom I want to release my anger, I have to go out of my way to find a person with whom to do the detour. A detour in the road has to be safe and passable; the person with whom I take the detour has to be safe, objective, clear and nonjudgmental. So, before coming directly to me with their complaint, criticism, or comments, my workshop participants are asked to take the detour to see what part of their feelings and thoughts may be connected to their recent or distant past.

After they take the detour, I then encourage them to speak to me directly and I will be glad to listen to everything they feel and have to say. Most of the time, however, thanks to the efficient employment of the questions posed by the person facilitating the Detour Method, participants almost never come to talk with me at all. They discover that their disproportionate reaction to what I said was more about them and their histories than it was about them and me in the present. (See Appendix for a description of the Detour Method and the complete eight-stage process of identifying anger, rage, regression.)

Should a participant still need to speak with me, it usually takes less than ten minutes and what is said is about him or her and me in the here and now. Very often when I listen, I realize that I owe the person an apology—and I make it.

Claudia, who is a born-again Christian, was outraged at several of the workshop participants for "taking the Lord's name in vain" while undergoing their deepest anger release work at my four-day anger intensive—Facing the Fire. Finally, she turned to my assistant and asked if she could speak to her about her concerns, because she was thinking about leaving this "un-Christian seminar." Karen Blicher has been assisting and cofacilitating with me for seventeen years in my PEER (primary, emotional, energy, recovery) training program for therapists and at the longer Facing the Fire intensives. Karen went out with Claudia and twenty minutes later returned with a smiling woman who was back fully in the present. Claudia completely understood that the other people's use of language would not hurt her or demean her in any way. She again was ready to participate, gladly, in the rest of the program, and didn't need to speak to me about it.

HOW THE DETOUR METHOD WORKS

Part 1

Karen began by giving Claudia her undivided attention and encouraging Claudia to tell her what she was feeling and thinking regarding the issue of people expressing their anger and using what to her was unacceptable language. Claudia immediately responded by saying she was outraged at all the cursing that had been going on and was scared of being hurt.

Part 2

Then Karen asked her if the cursing reminded her of anything, anyone or any events in her past. Karen told me she took about two minutes, and while doing so, she took deep full breaths and encouraged Claudia to do the same. Then

Claudia started crying and said, "It reminds me of my grandfather, who I spent several years with from twelve to eighteen after both my parents were killed in a car wreck. He was a great man and everybody loved him. But when he would drink he'd curse everyone out including my grandmother and me." Claudia went on to tell Karen that while her grandfather never hit her during his drunken tirades he did strike her grandmother more than a few times. Karen nodded her head up and down and continued to make eye contact with Claudia, encouraging her to take all the time she needed to tell this as Karen empathized with her. Claudia cried for several minutes. Karen offered her hand to hold and Claudia immediately took it.

Part 3

Karen then asked Claudia what she would have liked to say or do to her grandfather when he drank, swore and hurt her grandmother. Claudia took a few deep breaths and got really angry and said, "What I would have liked to say to him is, 'How can you act so holy and Christian one minute and act like the damn devil the next minute? Get some help and stop your damn drinking!'"

Karen squeezed her hand and said, "Good for you." Claudia, looking radiant and strong, said, "I can't believe I said that. I've wanted to say that for years. I realize I was angry at the people in the room and at John because they were getting to say and feel things I've never allowed myself to even think, much less say before."

I'm sure Karen smiled her warm smile.

Part 4

Karen asked, "What would you have liked for him to say or do back then?"

Claudia only took a moment and said, "I wish with my whole heart he would have said, 'I'm sorry and I'll get help and never hurt you or your grandmother again.'" Claudia let out a huge sigh of relief.

Part 5

Karen then asked her, "How are you feeling right now?"

"I feel much better now," Claudia answered. "I feel relaxed. I can't believe this. I haven't thought about this in years and years. I guess I'd just buried it until this workshop and watching those people do their work."

Part 6

"Okay, what do you need to say to John now?" Karen asked (almost knowing the answer because she has successfully completed the Detour Method with hundreds of folks over the years).

"Nothing really," Claudia responded. "John's just doing what we paid him for, and actually I just need to tell him how much I appreciate what he's helping to bring up."

Karen gave Claudia attention, empathy, time, contact, and facilitated emotional release or discharge of pent-up emotions from long ago that she never felt safe enough to feel and express before. By using the simple, easy to remember and very efficient Detour Method, Karen was able to help Claudia go back gently into her past, since she was already headed in that direction by way of her regression. Based on what Claudia was perceiving and experiencing in the workshop, Karen supported her to get some but not all of her feelings out.

Here is the play-by-play explanation of the Detour Method so you can choose to use it with people who have read this book or have attended one of the many Detour Method seminars held by me and my associates around the country.

- Ask the person what he is are feeling or thinking as he begins the process.
- Ask her what this experience, circumstance, person or place is reminding her of from her recent or distant past.
- Ask them what *they* would have liked to do or say back then. Encourage them to express this verbally and, if trained to do so, physically. (See list of PEER-trained people on my Web site.)
- Ask them what they would have liked said or done *to them* in the past.
- Ask them how they are feeling now.
- Ask them what they need to say or do in the present.

It is important to note that all of these are questions that adults tend to ask other adults. Regressed men and women, who are drowning in their histories, their fears and their anxieties, tend to make statements full of assumptions and advice.

Once you have done the Detour Method many times it is like anything else: you can deviate from the linear rules just set down and improvise—if you have been trained to do so and have been on the receiving end of the process yourself many times.

HOW DO YOU KNOW THE
DETOUR METHOD HAS WORKED?

After going through the detour process, the person usually takes a deep breath and sighs, which is a physical cue that says, "I'm back to my adult state."

The person usually feels and expresses gratitude to you for making it safe enough to do the process with him and for you seeing his feelings and not judging him.

While there have been no scientific studies done, I have asked hundreds of people how they feel after taking the detour. Ninety-nine percent say "better," "great," or "thank you for seeing and hearing me."

One of my best stories comes from Herman, a big burly guy from Ripley, Mississippi, who attended a daylong training on anger, regression and the Detour Method. He brought his son-in-law with him. Neither said much during the whole day so I didn't really know if they were getting anything useful out of the seminar at all. Then several weeks later I received a call from Herman.

"Damn, this stuff works," he started right off saying to me when I answered the phone.

"Who is this?" I asked.

"You probably don't remember me, but me and my son-in-law attended your workshop in Atlanta several weeks ago and I was very touched by the whole day. But I wasn't sure it wasn't just some New Age bullshit until me and the boy went fishing last week. I got this new fishing boat, boy is it a beauty, and I let him back it into the water and damned if he didn't back the thing right into the pier and put a huge dent into it. I got so pissed off I couldn't hardly see straight. I started cussing and fussing and he got defensive and started cussing me back. We finally got into the boat and cruised down the river not speaking to each other for about an hour when he said the thing that turned it all around and made it one of the greatest times we've ever had together."

He finally paused.

"What did he say to you, Herman?" I asked.

"Simply," Herman laughed and said, "Pop, you think we ought to do the Detour Method with each other and grow ourselves back up?" He asked me the questions you taught us and I realized that the dent in the boat was not the end of the world, and I got it that my Uncle Buck shamed me all the time about breaking things when I was a little boy when I would stay with him and Aunt Elsie. And my son-in-law regressed back to the time his father took him hunting and he lost his shotgun. We grew ourselves back up and I just wanted to call and tell you this damn stuff really works."

Once learned, practiced and used, the Detour Method will cut down misunderstanding, projecting, miscommunication, arguing, fighting, disagreeing and regretting by maybe 50 to 80 percent. When these behaviors are reduced, the need to medicate feelings goes down as well. The Detour Method may also cut down premature divorce by quite a bit by ensuring that you are divorcing your spouse, and not your parents or your ex-spouses all over again. It may diminish the number of employees you fire out of old rage instead of good reason. Using the Detour Method may help keep you from quitting a job before you are really prepared to do so—financially and emotionally. Taking the Detour Method often will increase your ability to stay in the present and to create and maintain a very important thing that reduces rage and anger incidents and feelings by 50 to 90 percent: setting strong and easy-to-defend boundaries.

6

SETTING BOUNDARIES AND KNOWING YOUR LIMITS

WHAT ARE BOUNDARIES?

BOUNDARIES ARE LINES THAT you draw in the sand, on the carpet, in the air, in your soul, in your body and in life in general. Others can't cross these lines without consequences and repercussions. A boundary is not imaginary, though you may not be able to see it. It says, "This is how close you can come to me—physically, emotionally, spiritually, financially, sexually and verbally."

Boundaries, if created and defended appropriately, will help prevent you from getting angry as often, because you will feel less violated, offended, abused or exhausted.

TYPES OF BOUNDARIES

Physical

Different cultures allow for differences in physical boundaries. The standard physical boundary for most Americans is about eighteen inches, depending on who we are, our relationship to the other persons, and how safe we feel or don't feel with them. Boundaries can also change—shorten or lengthen—based on how we feel at the moment.

Emotional

We will let others get close to us emotionally in direct proportion to our level of safety with them and our level of trust in the kind of relationship we have. Acquaintances can only get so close, friends a little closer, good friends closer, best friends very close. But all of these differ from the emotional closeness we might allow certain family members, lovers, husbands and wives.

Spiritual

We will only discuss our spirituality with those with whom we feel close. We might allow our minister, spiritual guide, priest or rabbi to come closer than, say, the person handing out spiritual pamphlets in the airport.

Financial

One person may know our money situation—our accountant, but not our father. We might tell our best friend about our financial situation, but not our son. On the other hand, our wife or husband may know everything about our financial life, but we may not completely trust our best friend with this information.

Sexual

We don't make love with someone we're not committed to. Or, perhaps we only make love with someone we have known and trusted for a certain length of time. We can make out but not go "all the way." We won't do certain things. We won't even be asked to do certain things. We only want to be held, regardless of the fact that fifteen minutes ago we made love.

Verbal

We will not be called names when we argue, but it is okay to do so when we are playing or not serious. We won't be criticized under any circumstances unless we ask for it. We won't be yelled at. We won't be shamed. We won't be compared to a past lover or spouse. We won't allow anyone to discuss our body, no matter who he or she is.

You have a right to set any boundaries that you need, and you have a right to change them as you feel safer or more trusting. No one can tell you that your boundary is unreasonable unless you ask that person—a therapist or sponsor, for example.

DEFENDING YOUR BOUNDARIES

The real problem with boundaries is that most people don't know how to defend them—when they finally realize they have to set them. An undefended boundary is not a boundary, but just another good personal growth or recovery idea.

Jason told me that he didn't have trouble setting boundaries but that most people didn't honor them. I asked him to give me an example. Jason said that when he goes home and sits down at the dinner table, his mother puts food on his plate.

"I tell her I don't want certain things, and she puts them on my plate anyway and says that I have to try them. I tell her I don't want to. I set a boundary but she doesn't pay any attention to it."

I told Jason that then this wasn't a boundary, and he argued for a couple of minutes that indeed it was and that she ignored it.

Exasperated, Jason finally said, "Okay, what can I do to make her honor my boundaries?"

"There are literally hundreds of possibilities," I answered. "You eat a meal before visiting your mom and tell her you're not eating. You take the food she puts on your plate, walk over to the garbage can and throw it away. You push back from the table. You get up and leave. The list is endless."

He looked at me, stunned. "I never thought of any of those before. I just thought that because she is my mom I shouldn't be rude."

Did I mention that Jason is thirty years old and finishing his doctorate in psychology?

When we can set and keep boundaries we will be less prone to anger and almost never enraged. The less we set and defend our boundaries, however, the more we will tend to get angry and end up feeling victimized, resentful and relapsing.

Yesterday, Robert, a very well-educated dentist who has been in private practice twenty years, came to see me for a consultation. During the hour he told me how his ex-wife "won't leave me alone. I tell her not to call or come by and she does anyway. I'm so angry I could kill her."

I listened and then asked if he would like my response. He said he would. I told him, "You know who I let in my house? Only the ones I want in. If they have a gun or a knife and want in, I will have to let them. If they don't and I let them in anyway, even if I don't want to, who is responsible?"

"But you're not listening to me," he returned. "I tell her not to call or come by and she shows up at my house anyway."

"She does, because she can. Because you have not set a boundary that you are prepared to defend."

"I wish I could just keep her out of my life instead of learning how to set a damn boundary. Why didn't someone teach me how to do this?"

Jason and Robert both thought they were setting boundaries, and they were using the right words, but their actions did not match their words. Most people who do not know about boundaries get very frustrated when discussing them because they tend to see only black and white—either I let my mother, ex-wife, etc., do what they want or I have to leave or go away. There are many ways to defend boundaries once we get clear about needing them in order to have healthy and functional relationships.

Here are a few ways to set and defend your boundaries. As I told Jason, there are literally dozens of things to do.

Go inside yourself, take a few deep breaths, and ask yourself, "What do I need in this situation or with this person?"

State your request/boundary clearly. For example, "I will not listen to racist or gay bashing jokes. If someone starts to tell one, I will say, 'Please stop. I'm not open to listening to these kinds of jokes.'" (Such "jokes," as I mentioned earlier, are a form of rage.)

If the person has not listened to your request, repeat it again.

Most people will honor your request. If they still refuse to comply, chances are you are dealing with someone who has no understanding of boundaries, frequently tramples other people's boundaries and is likely to be regressed. Such people need to be handled with extra care. Here are further steps you can take.

If the offense is verbal, you have several options. You can move to another part of the room, turn on a radio, talk over the person, or even stick your fingers in your ears and start humming. (This may seem juvenile, but you have permission to do whatever you need to protect your boundaries, provided you do not hurt yourself or anyone else.)

Leave the room for a few minutes.

If necessary, you may need to leave the house, party or work environment. A simple walk around the block can calm you and provide a new perspective on the situation.

You may have to get creative and think of a solution unique to the situation in which you find yourself. The important thing to remember is that you always have options, even if you elect not to use them. Situations where you are limited to the two options of tolerating the behavior or leaving are rare. Most solutions dwell in the gray area between the two.

BUILDING WALLS
VERSUS CREATING BOUNDARIES

When we can't, won't or don't know how to set boundaries, we still feel we have to do something. Very often we rage. Most alcoholics/addicts and the people who love them have been invaded, have listened to jokes they didn't want to hear, have had food piled on their plates . . . have been engulfed, dishonored, defiled, molested, beaten and incested so many times that, in order to survive, they have erected huge, thick walls, dug moats around them and filled the moats with crocodiles. No one is allowed to enter unless the drawbridge is let down.

These walls and crocodiles become the "resentments" alcoholics and addicts cannot afford to have. We learn to hide our emotions, feelings, sexuality, talent, needs, desires and truths behind the bricks and mortar, and then wonder why we don't have more intimacy, love, communication and connection in our lives. Every once in a while we remove a brick or two in our marriages or families. We might temporarily remove two hundred bricks when we first enter into a romance, but then six months later we replace the bricks and double the guards. We remove a few bricks when we have a few drinks and then deny that we did so the next day when sober. We may take down a whole section when we have a spiritual experience, but when we discover the minister ran off with the choir director, we immediately put the wall back in place, complete with barbed wire and broken glass on top.

How do you know your partner has a wall around him or her? Check to see if your head is flat from beating it against that wall a thousand or so times. We all want to take our walls down, but in order to do so someone has to teach us how to set and defend healthy boundaries. We have to learn to recognize our limits and then not go beyond them. We also have to feel and express appropriately the anger we have at all those who trespassed our boundaries in the past.

WHAT ARE LIMITS?

A limit is a statement coupled with consistent behavior that says how far I will go toward you—physically, emotionally, spiritually, financially and sexually—and go no further.

Cities post signs saying where their boundaries are—they are called the city limits—and speed limit signs are posted saying how fast we can go before we get a ticket. I wish people came with posted signs saying just where their life limits are, and how fast and far beyond them they are willing or not willing to go.

Some examples: On Susan's first date she will hold her date's hand but go no further. On her second date she will tell her date only a few things about her childhood. Not until the third or fourth date will she tell someone why she and her husband divorced. Michael will pray with his wife but will not pray in public. He will tell a dear friend how much money he has in his pocket, but he will not tell someone he barely knows how much he has in his savings account. Rebecca will make love to someone she has known for a year or more, but will not "hook up" with any of her fellow college students.

What makes so many alcoholics/addicts and the people who love them very angry and full of rage is that they do not know what their limits are. They are constantly speeding right past them until *life* pulls them over and hands them a ticket. A buddy of mine who was just recently divorced went out with a woman he met on the Internet. On their first date she asked him why he and his wife divorced. "I didn't want to tell her," he confessed to me, "but I told her and felt bad the rest of the evening. Why did I tell her when I didn't want to?" He was not used to setting limits and went further than he wanted to. And he was not used to setting boundaries and let her come into his personal space and history further than he was comfortable with.

Robin tried to set limits with her oldest son, now eighteen. She told him that if he didn't stop drinking and drugging he would end up in jail. She said she would bail him out only one time. It sounded like a limit, smelled like a limit, but it wasn't. She bailed him out three times within one year. When I asked her why she didn't stick to her limits and follow through, she replied, "He's my son. I couldn't leave him in jail. But I told him I'd never do it again." This young man now becomes someone who doesn't set limits and won't teach his children to set them. We have many children growing up angry because no one taught them how to set limits and follow through. Robin's words did not match her actions, and thus her son does not respect what she says. Instead he looks at what she does because she fears that he will get mad at her, leave her or stop loving her.

At the risk of being redundant I will repeat two main points: When people set and defend their boundaries they are not nearly as angry as often as those who don't. People who know and set their limits do not get nearly as angry because they know just how far to go, and the people *around* them also know how far they will and will not go.

Boundaries and limits increase the feeling of safety for everyone involved. Consistency—continuity plus congruency—equals greater comfort, better communication, and less anger, rage and confusion. It keeps men, women, children and pets less traumatized because there are fewer mixed messages and less meanness. Most importantly, people will not experience shock—the subject of our next chapter—as often as those without boundaries.

7

COMING OUT OF SHOCK AND INTO FEELING

WHAT IS SHOCK?

SHOCK IS A FROZEN, suspended-in-animation state. Our insides look like the famous Edvard Munch drawing *The Scream*, with the man standing on the bridge, his mouth gaping open at some horrific event witnessed or perhaps remembered after many years.

Many of us went into an emotional state of shock as a result of having our boundaries defiled as children, but we are also in shock about others' rages, withdrawals, abandonments and betrayals. We saw things done and heard things said that we couldn't believe were happening to us or to someone we loved. When we are in shock our bodies become rigid, our emotions become numb, and we stay that way for years—sometimes whole lifetimes. What we saw, heard and experienced traumatized us so thoroughly that when we think, feel or intuit that someone is about to become angry or enraged, we go back to the original time when someone did something similar, and we become the same people—very often children, but not always—that we were when we went into shock in the first place.

Shock is not a pathological state. Indeed, it is a state that allowed us to survive many traumas. However, though it was necessary at one time, shock is no longer a viable state for most adults to be in. When people are in a war zone, a car accident or other trauma, shock is necessary. And we stay in it until we feel safe enough to come out. Some of us never feel safe enough. Even though, objectively, it might well be safe, our bodies and souls don't feel this to be true.

In order to come completely out of shock and deal with the traumas that put us there in the first place, we have to do several things—and drinking and drugging are *not* among them. We may use alcohol, drugs, people and processes to perpetuate this shocked state and further numb us to our feelings and our memories of traumatic people, events, places and things.

First, we have to feel safe enough to come out of shock. Until the mid-1940s many men, women and children died of traumatic shock after major accidents and other disasters. No one could figure out how to save them until researchers discovered their patients needed more oxygen.

When a man, woman, child or animal goes into shock they have to be with safe people, in a safe place, and then receive lots of air into their bodies. When people go into shock the first thing they do is stop breathing, or they begin a lifetime of shallow breathing, taking in just enough oxygen to get by. Once we are in a safe space, we have to learn how to breathe again, taking in full deep breaths, filling the abdomen and exhaling with gusto and deliberateness.

Once we are in a safe place, breathing full deep breaths, then we will gradually, slowly—sometimes rapidly—begin to remember the traumas that put us in shock in the first place. These memories are usually so painful that if we are not with an experienced facilitator/guide/therapist we can retraumatize ourselves with the memory and return to the state of shock that we are trying to come out of. Luckily for us, the body will only allow us to come out of shock when we are *really* ready and not just because we tell ourselves, in our minds, that we are ready.

It is important to note that the mind is a very small portion of our complete memory bank. The body is the greater retainer of memory, and so it is important not to think we will recall the details of every trauma. Many people have experienced shocking things when they were too small to speak. Some have even experienced shock in the womb. Consequently, many people will not have the words they need when they finally do come out of shock. Instead, they will make sounds and let out sighs, screams, rage and tears.

Alcohol and drugs keep the body/mind numb and must be completely eliminated from the system before shock can be addressed fully and successfully. Not only is it important that we be free of these substances for a significant period, but also that we have a good deal of sobriety under our belts before trying to come out of shock. Recovering men and women who are also trying to recover their ability to feel need a support system thoroughly in place. Then, when these memories begin to come up, we will not drink or drug to push them back down. This is the main reason I strongly recommend that people have six months to a year minimum of clean and sober time before consciously attempting to come out of shock and to start dealing with the traumas that put us there in the first place.

WHAT HAPPENS WHEN
PEOPLE BEGIN TO COME OUT OF SHOCK?

Unless they have created a safe place and filled it with supportive, safe people, people coming out of shock will be very scared. If they have a safe place they will be a little fearful, but not so much that it impedes them from thawing out their frozen emotions. When this thawing occurs, feelings that have been in our deep freezers (bodies) begin coming up and out. Sadness, rage, anger, hurt and feelings of abandonment will pour out of us in direct proportion to how safe and ready we are to feel them. Our bodies have a wisdom of their own. Therefore, we can trust that when we've felt enough for the time being, our bodies will "tell" us by stopping the raging, sobbing and begin to reestablish equilibrium. Our bodies will prepare us to go back into our lives and assume our daily work, routines and responsibilities. Unfortunately, most people are afraid that if they ever come out of shock and start feeling all the feelings in them that this process will go on forever.

Hundreds of times I've heard the following statements

made by folks who are preparing to deal with traumas: "If I ever tap into my anger, I'll never come out and I'll destroy everything in sight," or "If I ever start crying, I'm afraid I'll never stop and I'll drown myself and everyone around me in my tears."

These are fears that sometimes are felt and other times are used as a way to keep from coming out of shock into feeling and healing.

When we come out of shock, we feel many different emotions. Likewise, the fact that we are feeling is the greatest evidence that we are coming out of emotional suspended animation.

Complete the following statement by checking the feeling you might have when you come out of shock.

When I Come Out of Shock, I Am Going to Feel . . .

✓ Anger   ✓ Hurt
✓ Rage   ✓ Peace
✓ Sadness   ✓ Joy
✓ Fear   ✓ Love
✓ Loneliness   ✓ Forgiveness

Chances are you will feel many of these at the same time. Indeed, you may feel all of them. Humans have the ability to experience many different feelings at the same time, while the brain is restricted to one thought at a time. By the way, these are all the feelings alcohol and drugs numb. As we shut down our anger and sadness, we also shut down peace, joy, love and forgiveness. Once we come out of shock, all our feelings are more readily available to us again, not just the ones we are afraid of.

HOW TO KNOW YOU
ARE COMING OUT OF SHOCK

People will come out of shock only in direct proportion to how safe they feel to do so. Here are the stages most people experience when coming out of shock:

- We begin to think about coming out of shock, usually because we are feeling safe and have created a safe environment to begin experiencing our repressed, buried feelings.
- We begin to think that it's finally safe enough to come out of shock. We are not sure, but we are now open to being shown it's okay to move back into our emotions.
- We begin to move from thinking to feeling. We are not quite there yet, but we are becoming aware of the safe people and surroundings in our life that might allow us to emerge from emotional hibernation.
- We finally feel safe enough to come out of shock, so we do so very gradually, allowing at first only the smallest amount of feelings to emerge.
- We are completely safe enough to come out of shock fully around certain issues we have never felt before. Note that we are not out of shock on every issue, but simply the ones we are ready to feel, heal and deal with.

- Feelings such as anger, sadness, fear, hurt, relief, joy and ecstasy are some of the feelings that will be displayed by us when we are fully out of shock.

All alcoholics, addicts and the people who love them will naturally have anger. When they stop numbing their feelings and come out of shock, their feelings and emotions will come alive again. If they don't stop numbing their feelings, however, the anger turns into rage and the rage turns into resentment. Alcoholism/addiction is resentment acted out and keeps the cycle of shock going—generation after generation.

8

ANGRY AT GOD

MOST ALCOHOLICS, ADDICTS AND the people who love them have a deep well of anger at God. However, quite a few are afraid to get angry with the Divine. It's one thing to feel anger at our moms, dads, ex's, bosses, etc., yet another thing entirely to have strong feelings of anger toward the Almighty. This mostly unconscious anger at God comes out at the people we love, our pets, the police and politicians. In psychology it is called displacement.

There are as many different reasons for being angry with God as there are people but we have been taught it's "not nice to get angry with God." One of the reasons I used to be angry with God was because for twenty-five years I suffered with almost terminal insomnia. I could only get "foxhole sleep"

—the kind soldiers get while in the middle of a battle. My personal battleground was my home as a child. I had to keep one eye open for incoming "artillery." I tossed and turned, took everything sold over the counter for sleep aid, and finally turned to alcohol, my trusty old friend, to help me get to sleep. At first it only took a beer or two and then a high-ball or two, then a pint or two, and then a quart or two.

One evening, up at the Boundary Waters in Minnesota, I was co-leading a men's wilderness retreat with a good friend, facilitator and part-time rabbi, Joe Lauer. He was conducting what he called "God Wrestling." He was working with a man who had lots of anger in him, and Joe finally got him to admit that a good deal of it was at God for allowing him to be born into a family that physically and emotionally abused him severely as a child. Joe picked up a limb from the ground that was about three or four inches in diameter and about five feet long. Joe asked the gentle man to take it, strike the ground and tell God how angry he felt toward him. Well, to make a long story short, Joe gave him not only plenty of support and encouragement but ample opportunity. After about twenty minutes the man said, "I can't get angry at God. It's just not right."

During that whole twenty minutes I was pacing around the circle of men, getting more and more angry and hoping like hell this guy would take the stick and wail into the night sky his and my own anger at God so I wouldn't have to. Joe was about to put the limb down when suddenly, without forethought, I jumped into the circle and said to Joe, "Give me that damn limb. I'm angry as hell at God." I took the limb and started pounding on the ground like the ape in the opening of the movie *2001*. My animal anger came pouring out at having been beaten and abused, at never knowing when in the night my father might jerk me out of bed and whip me for some minor offense committed earlier in the day and, most of all, for feeling God had abandoned me a long time ago. For twenty minutes I raged and wept, raged and wept, cursed and damned God. (Now I realize this was a way of praising him.)

Finally, I fell into a little heap on the ground, the men encircled me and Joe asked me what I needed. I said, "To be picked up and carried to my cabin and to have someone sleep on the porch all night so I won't be disturbed." They picked me up like a sack of potatoes, carried me to my bunk and laid me down, and I slept for fourteen hours straight—something I hadn't done more than once or twice in my life. It wasn't long after that that my insomnia disappeared, and it hasn't returned as of this writing. I sleep very well almost every night, and even the not-so-great nights are great compared to what they used to be. Coincidence? I know it isn't. My God didn't create any such thing as coincidence.

I believe my Higher Power not only invented anger, sadness, fear, love and joy, but is also quite capable of hearing all my feelings and is great enough, big enough and loving enough to absorb them all. As I've said many times, anger expressed appropriately equals energy, serenity and intimacy, not only with people but the Great Divine.

THE SPIRITUAL ELEMENT
IN REGRESSION AND ANGER

I don't know enough about spiritual matters so I won't take up much of your time here. Besides, the very word "spiritual" may send some into a regression, hurling them back to a hard pew in church somewhere forty years ago. But I do know regression is a gift to me from God. I believe God wants us to heal, so he sends us people, situations and circumstances that force us to look at our histories and deal with the past pain that we have kept pent up way too long. If we don't get it the first dozen times, God will send us a dozen more situations or husbands or wives or lovers to help us get closure on the feelings and facts that have been hiding in our brains and bodies for years, if not decades. There is grace in regression. Sometimes the grace is not seen for a long time.

I remember when I first went into AA. Whenever I heard someone say he was a "grateful alcoholic," I wanted to puke. Now I *am* one of those people. Alcoholism is a regression, and recovery can lead us into our histories by doing the Twelve Steps—especially steps four, five, nine and ten. Here we take an inventory of our past and then receive attention, empathy, time and contact from a sponsor as we share with them our insights, feelings and history. Regression is God's way of taking us back and helping us come out of the trances we live and die in.

ONE FINAL THOUGHT
ABOUT ANGER, RAGE AND REGRESSION

Alcohol, drugs, people, and Ben & Jerry's ice cream are all much more accessible than our anger, acceptance and love. I encourage you who are reading this to put down the alcohol and drugs when you are ready, put down the eighty-hour work week, give up the nicotine and compulsive sex, and—all right, you don't have to give up Ben & Jerry (but try to moderate your intake of that delicious Cherry Garcia). Then find some safe people and a safe place and open up your body bag full of anger, rage, sadness. Let them all out so there will be more room for joy, ecstasy (not the drug), laughter and love.

Learn to trust that the deeper you go into any feeling, such as anger, the deeper you will experience love and joy and perhaps, just perhaps, finally feel forgiveness and connection to all things past and present, dead or alive. Trust that you will come alive like you've never been before and live more fully in the here and now. With work, time, practice, patience and prayer you will learn to make the moment your safe home, create safe havens for all your loved ones and experience the peace that has been missing from your recovery.

APPENDIX

QUICK OVERVIEW OF KEY INFORMATION ON ANGER, RAGE, REGRESSION AND THE DETOUR METHOD

The Difference Between Rage and Anger

- **Rage** is a behavior or action designed to numb feelings such as sadness, fear and even anger. It usually causes pain to the one raging or the one receiving the rage.
- **Anger** is just a feeling (neither negative nor positive), and if expressed appropriately will not hurt anyone.

The Four Styles of Rage

- The Interrogator: fires lightning fast questions; is aggressive and bullying.
- The Intimidator: is full of "sound and fury"; very loud and overbearing.

- The Martyr (Poor Me): hides behind clouds of disappointment and fear, appearing to be the victim, but is as angry as anyone can be.
- The Distancer: runs for cover but returns later with greater strength, or leaks passive-aggressive rain on everyone.

Nine Things People Do When They Think They're Expressing Anger:

1. Shame
2. Blame
3. Demean
4. Demoralize
5. Criticize
6. Preach
7. Teach
8. Judge
9. Analyze

These are all inappropriate behaviors or actions that can elicit defensiveness or other unwanted, nonproductive behavior.

The Red Flags of Regression

- Raging and hysterics (feeling or being out of control)
- Distorted or unreal time (time passes very quickly or too slowly)
- Cold hands or feet

- Perspiring excessively
- Lump in your throat
- Dry mouth
- Heart beating wildly
- Knot in stomach
- Talking without really saying anything
- Not talking enough (going silent)
- Feeling like you don't have a choice (adults always have a choice)
- Thinking you always know best
- Feeling that you can't or shouldn't ask for help

Five Things That Will Grow You Back Up

1. Attention
2. Empathy
3. Time
4. Contact
5. Release

Five Questions to Ask Someone Who Wants to Take the Detour with You

1. What are you feeling and thinking right now?
2. Does what happened remind you of anything in your past?
3. What would you like to have said or done back then, but couldn't for any reason? If so, say it now.
4. What would you like to have seen happen or have said to you?

5. How are you feeling and thinking *now*? Do you still need to go talk to that person?

A Checklist to See If You Have Moved through Your Anger

- The event, person or place no longer occupies space in your head.
- You no longer need to talk about it to release your pent-up feelings.
- You don't beat up yourself about it and you don't need to beat up, physically or imaginatively, someone else.
- When you think about the event or person, you can "breathe easily."
- You forget what you were mad about in the first place.
- Something that would have triggered you in the past no longer does so.
- Your thinking is very clear about the person or event.
- You tend more toward gratitude for the experience.
- You don't hold a grudge or resentment—you've let go and let God.
- You may even feel forgiveness toward the person, place or thing.
- You don't need to drink or drug or medicate your feelings about it anymore. (You may drink and drug over something else, but not this.)

More from the author

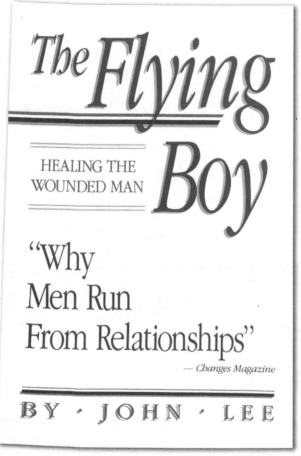

Code #0066 • $7.95

The Flying Boy is a book for all men
and women who are ready for some fresh insights
into their past and their pain.
